"Cramer and Werntz brilliantly move t
tian nonviolence beyond Yoder to sho
proaches, which often diverge from and challenge one another.
Not a typology with winners and losers, this book is rather an
invitation to further discernment and debate, and an aid to the
practical wisdom needed to follow Christ in a violent world.
This book is much needed and splendidly done."

—**William T. Cavanaugh**, DePaul University

"In a world torn apart by racism, sexism, militarism, and other
types of violence, this book offers a beacon of hope and profound insight. It unveils the rich diversity of the Christian pacifist
tradition in a style that is both elegant and engaging. Truly a
must read!"

—**Andrew Prevot**, Boston College

"This is a wonderful survey of the many ways in which the gospel of peace has been interpreted and enacted nonviolently. I
found the eight models helpful both for understanding varying
approaches to nonviolence and as a tool for self-inquiry and
spiritual discernment. I will be recommending the book to students and friends."

—**Nancy E. Bedford**, Garrett-Evangelical Theological Seminary

"With unusual nuance and insight, Cramer and Werntz identify
eight forms of Christian nonviolence, bringing to life its ecclesial
and spiritual depth. They also magnify the political and transformative voice of nonviolence, illustrating how its inspiration
and effects reach far beyond the church. A new and important
note for standard accounts of Christian pacifism resounds in
the chapter on Christian antiviolence. This creative yet historically grounded volume is a valuable addition to the war and
peace literature, easily accessible and captivating to students,
yet with an originality that will take theological scholarship on
nonviolence into new territory."

—**Lisa Sowle Cahill**, Boston College

A FIELD GUIDE TO CHRISTIAN NONVIOLENCE

KEY THINKERS, ACTIVISTS, *and* MOVEMENTS
for the Gospel *of* Peace

DAVID C. CRAMER *and* MYLES WERNTZ

Baker Academic
a division of Baker Publishing Group
Grand Rapids, Michigan

To our families:
Sarah, Eliot, and Arthur,
and Andrea, Wesley, and Liza

Published by Baker Academic
a division of Baker Publishing Group
PO Box 6287, Grand Rapids, MI 49516-6287
www.bakeracademic.com

Library of Congress Cataloging-in-Publication Data
Names: Cramer, David C., author. | Werntz, Myles, author.
Title: A field guide to Christian nonviolence : key thinkers, activists, and movements for the gospel of peace / David C. Cramer and Myles Werntz.
Description: Grand Rapids, Michigan : Baker Academic, a division of Baker Publishing Group, [2022] | Includes bibliographical references and index.
Identifiers: LCCN 2021023569 | ISBN 9781540960122 (paperback) | ISBN 9781540965288 (casebound) | ISBN 9781493434732 (ebook)
Subjects: LCSH: Nonviolence—Religious aspects—Christianity
Classification: LCC BT736.6 .C73 2022 | DDC 241/.697—dc23
LC record available at https://lccn.loc.gov/2021023569

Scripture quotations are from the New Revised Standard Version of the Bible, copyright © 1989 National Council of the Churches of Christ in the United States of America. Used by permission. All rights reserved.

Baker Publishing Group publications use paper produced from sustainable forestry practices and post-consumer waste whenever possible.

22   23   24   25   26   27   28   7   6   5   4   3   2   1

CONTENTS

7. Liberationist Nonviolence

8. Christian Antiviolence

PREFACE

This little book is two decades in the making. On September 11, 2001, the two of us were just a couple weeks into the fall semester of our respective academic programs—David as a freshman Bible and philosophy major in Indiana and Myles as a second-year seminarian in Texas. As young, white evangelicals, neither of us had thought deeply about the relationship between violence and our Christian faith. With the collapse of the World Trade Center towers came the collapse of our innocence.

We were sent back to Scripture with new questions and new lenses. Jesus's Sermon on the Mount (Matt. 5–7) took on a new sense of urgency. When Jesus said to "love your enemies and pray for those who persecute you" (5:44), did he have in mind those who are intent on killing you? And when he said not to "resist an evildoer" (5:39), did that entail refusing to engage in violence for personal or national defense? Such questions sent us searching for answers, not only in Scripture but also in Christian theology and ethics.

As with many evangelicals looking for answers to questions about violence and the Christian faith, we were directed to the writings of one of the most prominent and prolific Christian pacifists of the twentieth century, John Howard Yoder. Our interests in Yoder's work on nonviolence led us each to pursue doctorates in theology and ethics at Baylor University in Waco, Texas, where we met in 2011, when David was first entering the program and Myles was beginning his final year. At Baylor, we each wrote dissertations dealing with Christian nonviolence in which Yoder featured prominently and published a number of other works that directly or indirectly promoted Yoder's writings.[1]

In the meantime, a number of survivor advocates were working to bring to light the long history of Yoder's sexual violence toward women—a history that for decades had been minimized or conveniently overlooked by male scholars like us who were drawn to Yoder's arguments for Christian nonviolence. In 2013, Mennonite mental health clinician and pastoral theologian Ruth Krall published a collection of essays providing an in-depth case study of Yoder's sexual violence and the Mennonite Church's response. That same year, Mennonite theater professor, survivor, and survivor advocate Barbra Graber wrote an essay titled "What's to Be Done about John Howard Yoder?" which struck a nerve in the Mennonite world and beyond. An avalanche of testimonies of and responses to Yoder's sexual violence ensued, and once again, our innocence—this time about our own complicity in propagating the work of a known sexual predator—collapsed.[2]

The revelations about Yoder caused us to scrutinize the foundations of our commitments to Christian nonviolence. If one

1. See Werntz, *Bodies of Peace*; Cramer, "Theopolitics." See also Werntz, "Erase This from the Blackboard"; Cramer, "Evangelical Hermeneutics, Anabaptist Ethics." Myles was also involved in editing two posthumous works of Yoder; see J. Yoder, *Nonviolence—A Brief History*; J. Yoder, *Revolutionary Christianity*.

2. For an annotated timeline of Yoder's life and a bibliography of writings about Yoder's sexual violence, see Krall, "John Howard Yoder."

of the leading twentieth-century voices for Christian nonviolence was himself violent in such heinous ways, is Christian nonviolence itself a sham?

Instead of leading us to reject our commitments to Christian nonviolence, this time of questioning and scrutinizing led us to broaden our understanding of nonviolence and deepen our commitments to it—even as our convictions were transformed in light of what we learned. We found that Yoder's own approach to nonviolence has precedents in figures like André and Magda Trocmé, who were inspired by Jesus's revolutionary nonviolence to nonviolently resist the Nazis and the Vichy government by harboring thousands of Jewish refugees in the small French town where André pastored. Moreover, we came to see Christian nonviolence not as a unified, coherent position but as a dynamic, multivalent tradition that includes a number of identifiable streams—not all of which are entirely compatible with one another. We came to see that this multifaceted tradition includes mystics and liberationists, socialists and anarchists, Catholics and Methodists, in addition to Mennonites focused on discipleship.

Yet in our conversations about Christian nonviolence with others—both those committed to Christian nonviolence and those opposed to it—we often heard it described in a fairly limited way as nonviolence of Christian discipleship. This is the view that Christians practice nonviolence because Jesus taught us to and exemplified it in his own life, which serves as a model for Christian disciples. It is also the view that Yoder both popularized and provided scholarly credibility to through his many writings but especially his 1972 work, *The Politics of Jesus.* Even now, when we self-identify as Christian pacifists or advocates of Christian nonviolence, we often find ourselves pigeonholed as "Yoderians" and our view described as the "Yoder-Hauerwas" position, which combines Yoder's approach with that of his friend and colleague Stanley Hauerwas—another prominent pacifist of the twentieth and twenty-first centuries.

In 2016, out of frustration with this pigeonholing, David wrote an essay for *Sojourners* magazine titled "A Field Guide to Christian Nonviolence." That essay identifies eight different streams of Christian nonviolence and discusses a representative figure for each. The headline for the article reads, "There are different ways to understand the gospel's call to peace—and that's a good thing."

Around that same time, Myles appeared on a panel on the ethics of war where he was the representative for Christian pacifism, which the other panelists pigeonholed as the Yoder-Hauerwas position. Having read the *Sojourners* essay, he suggested to David that we expand it into a book, where instead of identifying just one representative of each stream, we would include the many thinkers, activists, and movements that compose each stream.

After five years of research and writing, sending chapters back and forth, and soliciting feedback from trusted friends and scholars—all of which took place in the midst of a number of moves and job changes in our lives, deep political turmoil at a national level, and a deadly pandemic at the global level—*A Field Guide to Christian Nonviolence* has finally come to fruition. We offer it in the hope that it will lead to better understanding of this tradition by proponents and opponents alike—and in so doing will contribute in some small way to the gospel of peace.

David C. Cramer and Myles Werntz

ACKNOWLEDGMENTS

We have many people to thank for their role in making this book a reality. We would first like to thank the team at *Sojourners* for their inspiration for this project and for their permission to adapt a 2016 essay into this book by the same name. We also thank the team at Baker Academic, especially our acquisitions editor, Dave Nelson, who believed in this project from the beginning, and our project editor, Melisa Blok, who ably guided the project to completion.

One of the risks of writing a survey like this is that you miss the trees for the forest. While we each have spent a lot of time researching and writing on Christian nonviolence, we make no claims to be experts on each of the streams we describe in this book. We therefore owe a huge debt of gratitude to the experts in the various areas who reviewed our chapters. In particular, we thank Susannah Larry and Drew Strait for reviewing chapter 1; Eli McCarthy for reviewing chapter 2; Paul Harvey and Andrew Prevot for reviewing chapter 3; Ry Siggelkow for reviewing chapter 4; Janna Hunter-Bowman for reviewing chapter 5; Malinda Elizabeth Berry, Russell Johnson, and Kyle Lambelet for reviewing chapter 6; Daniel Schipani and Matthew Whelan for reviewing chapter 7; and Leah Thomas and Hilary Scarsella for reviewing chapter 8. They each provided helpful critiques and suggestions from their respective area of expertise, which greatly improved the manuscript. Where we were unable to provide the level of nuance they suggested, we recommend that readers look up their work. Of course, all remaining deficiencies in the text are ours.

Special thanks to the Mennonite Historical Library at Goshen College, Indiana, for the 2018 Schafer-Friesen Research Fellowship that helped to fund research for this project. Thanks as well to our institutional homes for their support during the writing of this manuscript: Logsdon Seminary at Hardin-Simmons University and Abilene Christian University for Myles, and Anabaptist Mennonite Biblical Seminary for David. We would also like to thank the Religion Department at Baylor University, especially Paul Martens, Jonathan Tran, Barry Harvey, and Natalie Carnes.

Additional thanks to the many people who have been instrumental in this journey for us. I (Myles) would like to thank Robert Ellis, my dean at Logsdon Seminary who supported my writing, and former students and colleagues who have been instrumental in helping me wrestle through these questions—in particular, Andrew Black, Josh Carpenter, Ryan Gladwin, Claire Hein Blanton, Craig Hovey, Kyle B. T. Lambelet, Wyatt Miles, and Crystal Sullivan.

I (David) would like to thank Beverly Lapp, my dean at Anabaptist Mennonite Biblical Seminary, who supported this project; Timothy Paul Erdel, my mentor who first introduced me to Christian nonviolence; Andrew Whitehead, my longtime friend and coconspirator; and the good people of Hope Fellowship in Waco, Texas, and Keller Park Church in South Bend, Indiana, especially my copastor, Carrie Badertscher, and longtime board chair, Joel Boehner. I also thank the members of my Mennonite retreat group—Mark Baker, Bob Brenneman, Jamie Pitts, John Roth, and Ryan Schellenberg—for their helpful feedback on early drafts and encouragement throughout the project. And I thank the students in my Christian Attitudes toward War, Peace, and Revolution course at Anabaptist Mennonite Biblical Seminary over the past few years for thoughtfully engaging early drafts of chapters: Evan Beck, Alejandra Garcia Baez, Pratik Bagh, Shabnam Bagh, Joel Beachy, Quinn Brenneke, Kevin Chupp, John Glassbrenner, Zane Griggs, Daniel Koons, Laura Kraybill, Sibonokuhle Ncube, Patrick James Obonde, Andy Oliver, Matthew Peterson, Lindsay Ralph, Emily Ritchey, Sarah Schlegel, Karsten Snitker, Adam Stultz, Luis Marcos Tapia, Hank Unruh, and the cohort of students from Meserete Kristos College in Bishoftu, Ethiopia.

Finally, we would each like to thank our families for their support for and patience with this project. I (Myles) am grateful to my spouse, Sarah, and children, Eliot and Arthur. I (David) am grateful to my spouse, Andrea, and children, Wesley and Liza. We could not have done this without you, and it is to you we dedicate this book, with much love and appreciation.

Introduction

Christian nonviolence has a long and storied legacy, one that begins in the earliest days of the church, as figures like Tertullian, Origen, and Athenagoras offered their defense of the Christian position toward the Roman military: nonparticipation.[1] Though hardly offering a full-blown theory of nonviolence, these early witnesses articulated a bedrock presumption about the relationship between Christians and violence that would be developed, altered, and debated over the next two millennia. During this period, presumptions about how to define and identify violence and whether Christians could join the military or engage in any acts of violence for personal defense or defense of the helpless all underwent scrutiny as the shape of violence changed.

In the twentieth century, Christian ethicists and theologians explored the contours of this topic as new questions surfaced: What is the aim of nonviolence? Does one have to be a Christian to practice nonviolence? How do those committed to nonviolence engage the social structures that support and create the

---

1. See Kalantzis, *Caesar and the Lamb*.

conditions for violence? With the emergence of new challenges such as nuclear weapons, global terrorism, and increasing recognition of sexual and gender-based violence and of social structures that perpetuate violence, the scholarship around Christian nonviolence has evolved to address new concerns and challenges.

Our thesis is this: Christian nonviolence has never been monolithic but has always included merging and diverging streams; it is therefore best understood as a dynamic and contested tradition rather than a unified and settled position. Over the last five years, as we have been invited to sit on panels on Christianity and violence and engage in discussions around Christian nonviolence in the church and academy, the predominant assumption we have repeatedly encountered is that all arguments for nonviolence are the same. And frequently, popular understandings of Christian nonviolence are summed up by the equivalent of a modern-day version of the Schleitheim Confession, the sixteenth-century Anabaptist document that draws a sharp line between the "perfection of Christ" and the world, with the former characterized by its renunciation of the sword and the latter characterized by its use of the sword.[2] Such a characterization of Christian nonviolence is mistaken in at least two ways. First, it assumes that all contemporary Anabaptists adhere to the Schleitheim Confession. (They do not.)[3] And, second, it assumes that all contemporary advocates and practitioners of Christian nonviolence are like Anabaptists. (They are not.) But when the only version of Christian nonviolence you are presented is the Schleitheim Confession, all forms of Christian nonviolence tend to look and sound like

2. See Sattler, "Schleitheim Articles."

3. For discussions of the various forms of nonviolence and pacifism among Mennonites in particular, see Burkholder and Gingerich, *Mennonite Peace Theology*; Cramer, "Mennonites & Pacifism."

traditional Mennonite nonresistance.[4] As we described in the preface, this pigeonholing is due in no small part to the prominence of Mennonite theologian John Howard Yoder, whose arguments for nonviolence loomed large in the academy and in popular imagination for nearly half a century, obscuring other forms of Christian nonviolence that already existed and other voices for Christian nonviolence that were developed during that same period.[5]

There are a number of anthologies of historic writings on Christian nonviolence, but they tend to pay little attention to the distinctions within the broad tradition and how the various approaches to Christian nonviolence either complement or diverge from one other. Likewise, there are many constructive arguments for Christian nonviolence—including by each of us—but frequently they are singularly focused on a specific form of violence or on specific rationales for nonviolence. As we surveyed the literature on Christian nonviolence, we could find no recent text to introduce Christian nonviolence to those interested in learning about its nuances and varieties.[6]

So we wrote one.

This book is not an apologetic for Christian nonviolence. Experience has taught us that arguments for and against nonviolence rarely change the mind of the one holding the contrary view. We do not aim, therefore, to convince non-pacifist Christians to become pacifists by reading this book. Rather,

4. *Nonresistance* refers here to a specific form of nonviolence, patterned closely off the Sermon on the Mount, in which Christians refrain from retribution, endure unjust suffering, and do not cooperate with violence. But unlike other forms of nonviolence we discuss, nonresistance does not entail an active response and instead emphasizes non-cooperation with violence.

5. This monolithic view of Christian nonviolence also fails to recognize that Yoder's own approach to nonviolence diverged from the Schleitheim Confession and developed over time. On this development, see Cramer, "Realistic Transformation."

6. The most recent work in this genre is J. Yoder, *Nevertheless*, originally published in 1971 and updated in 1992.

our goal is to invite both pacifists and non-pacifists—and all those in between—to encounter a dynamic, living and breathing tradition within the broader tradition of Christianity. As we describe, the tradition of Christian nonviolence is flawed and at times even harmful, but at other times it can also be life-giving and inspiring, regardless of whether one is part of it.

In the following chapters, we describe eight major streams of Christian nonviolence. These streams are not meant to be mutually exclusive but often overlap or diverge in interesting and instructive ways. With just a few exceptions, we use thinkers and activists to illustrate a particular stream that represents their primary orientation to nonviolence, even if they also use other forms of reasoning in various places. We discuss Martin Luther King Jr. in chapter 6 as a representative of nonviolence as political practice, for example, while recognizing that he was a complex figure whose work involved both mystical dimensions (chapter 3) and liberationist tendencies (chapter 7). Likewise, we discuss Catholic Worker cofounder Dorothy Day and Protestant ethicist Stanley Hauerwas in terms of their emphasis on nonviolence as Christian virtue in chapter 2, while acknowledging that they at times describe nonviolence using apocalyptic language and categories (chapter 4) as well. In describing the complexity and multiplicity of Christian nonviolence, we do not intend to minimize the complexity and multiplicity of individual thinkers and activists. We all use multiple forms of reasoning and argumentation for our views—sometimes even forms that are mutually contradictory. Such is the human condition.

As we discuss in the following chapters, the Christian realist Reinhold Niebuhr distinguished between two forms of pacifism or nonviolence that he witnessed in his day: (1) a more inward-focused, quietist, absolutist, communalist pacifism that focuses on faithfulness and fidelity to Jesus's teachings on nonresistance and in so doing offers a witness to the world of another kingdom without trying to change the world, and (2) a more outward-focused, activist, political pacifism that takes Jesus's teachings less literally and focuses instead on the effectiveness of nonviolence, using nonviolence as a tool for social change and political transformation in the world. Niebuhr considered the first kind of pacifism to be useful as a reminder of the ideal of God's kingdom but generally irrelevant when it comes to making the kinds of relative judgments that are necessary when Christians enter the political realm. He considered the second kind of pacifism to be not only misguided but also *heretical* both in terms of its fidelity to Christian Scriptures and tradition and in terms of its empirical claims to effectiveness.[7]

Niebuhr's distinction has persisted in the popular imagination, as the first, communal kind of nonviolence has come to be associated with names like Yoder and Hauerwas, and the second, political kind of nonviolence has come to be associated with King (and, beyond Christianity, with Mohandas Gandhi). We intentionally structured the chapters with this distinction in mind, beginning with four streams more often associated with the first type and ending with four streams more often associated with the second type. But, while this distinction is not wholly meritless, our contention is that it blurs and breaks down considerably when the full picture of each stream is appreciated. Is it less political, for example, to harbor Jewish refugees from Nazis or to burn Vietnam War draft cards than it is to march on Selma or to practice just peacemaking initiatives? While these actions are done with differing theological and ethical motivations and considerations, which we describe

7. See Niebuhr, "Why the Christian Church Is Not Pacifist."

in the following chapters, they do not always fall neatly along the lines marked out by Niebuhr.

We invite readers, as they make their way through this book, to view our descriptions as starting points—introductions to major thinkers, activists, and movements that coalesce around eight major approaches. It is our view that because violence appears in many guises, it must be confronted in many different ways. It is therefore not an argument against Christian nonviolence to recognize and acknowledge that the refusal to engage in violence takes a number of forms within the body of Christ. Not all approaches are compatible, and important arguments are often evoked when they diverge. But together, these eight streams provide a broad palette of arguments and insights about violence in the world and what it means for Christians to confront that violence and live faithfully amid it.

It is our conviction that Christian nonviolence, at its best, does not promise to end all wars or permanently settle all disputes. Rather, Christian nonviolence is an exercise of Christian wisdom, guided by the Spirit, who transforms our minds so that *we* "may discern what is the will of God—what is good and acceptable and perfect" (Rom. 12:2). It is in the spirit of marking out the pluriform ways in which this discernment takes place—retrieving and putting to good use the work of these many thinkers, activists, and movements—that we offer this book.

Nonviolence of Christian Discipleship

FOLLOWING JESUS IN A WORLD AT WAR

During the Second World War, the small mountainous village of Le Chambon, France, became a refuge for nearly five thousand Jews and other persons fleeing the Holocaust.[1] In a biography of André Trocmé, pastor and leader of the movement in Le Chambon, the biographer asks, "How is it that the population in Le Chambon and the surrounding area almost unanimously embraced the rescue effort?"[2] It is one thing to celebrate a radical individual, but how does this kind of group action emerge? In answering this question, we encounter a particular kind of Christian nonviolence: *nonviolence of Christian discipleship.*

1. For a full account, see Hallie, *Lest Innocent Blood Be Shed*; Schott, *Love in a Time of Hate.*
2. Chalamet, *Revivalism and Social Christianity*, 143.

Today, nonviolence of Christian discipleship—sometimes called *ecclesiocentric nonviolence*—is one of the most well-known forms of Christian nonviolence. This form emphasizes the role of the gathered Christian community—or, more properly, Christian disciples—in Christian nonviolence. According to this stream, nonviolence is a way of living in the world, shaped by reading of the Scriptures, corporate worship, and the practices of life together. Christian nonviolence is a habit of regular discipleship, which then becomes the mode of engagement in times of conflict.

As we describe below, nonviolence of Christian discipleship was popularized in the second half of the twentieth century by the works of John Howard Yoder, particularly his 1972 book, *The Politics of Jesus*. However, subsequent to the publication of this book, survivors and advocates exposed details of Yoder's own sexual violence toward women, including his colleagues and students.[3] This undermines any straightforward appropriation of this stream of nonviolence for today. In this chapter, then, we complicate the narrative by not only discussing Yoder's contributions to this stream but also exploring sources of this stream that predate Yoder (in figures like André Trocmé and Dietrich Bonhoeffer) and divergences within this stream among contemporary theologians and biblical scholars. According to this approach, the Christian community is called to be a nonviolent community that reads the Scriptures canonically in light of the nonviolent Jesus's call to Christian discipleship. The question that arises is whether a church can be called a church without this commitment to—and practice of—nonviolence. Thus, any failure to practice nonviolence threatens to undermine this approach on its own terms.

3. See our discussion in the preface.

The Nonviolent Revolution of Jesus

When André Trocmé's *Jesus and the Nonviolent Revolution* first appeared in English in 1972, it created a stir. Written by the pastor of the French Reformed Church of Le Chambon-sur-Lignon, the book offers a reading of the Gospels that draws on biblical scholarship to make the case for nonviolence as the way of the communities that Jesus founded. In taking up this topic, Trocmé largely sets aside the question of canonical progression: for Trocmé, it matters little whether the Hebrew Bible commends nonviolence, for he unapologetically embraces the view that "Jesus *is* the central event of history, because *de facto* his coming changed humankind."[4] Trocmé then connects the churches of Jesus to the ethic of Jesus on precisely this point: to be a disciple of Jesus is not simply to confess faith in Jesus but also to follow Jesus in the way of the cross.

For Trocmé, it is not enough to say that Jesus's *example* is one of nonviolence. Instead, Jesus's very substance as the *goel* (the mediator between the community and God) is of this nature: Jesus's mediation between God and humanity occurs in a way that abolishes whatever violence was present in Israel. "For the Christian, the figure of the 'Servant of Yahweh,' who gives his life in ransom for the guilty ones fallen into slavery, now thrusts itself upon Jesus (Mark 10:45). In this way, the law of retaliation was transmuted. Its demand for justice, for holiness, could never be abolished. But God's vengeance would now be borne by God himself, by the God who is the *goel* of his people in the person of his Son."[5]

For Trocmé, the way in which Jesus mediates for humanity and the way in which the church is connected to Christ morally and to the world in witness are integrally related. They are a

---

4. Trocmé, *Jesus and the Nonviolent Revolution*, xix.
5. Trocmé, *Jesus and the Nonviolent Revolution*, 11.

sacramental matrix of divine imitation, in which the church follows in the way of Jesus, for it is in this way that Jesus joins us to God the Father.

Over the course of the book, Trocmé unpacks the Hebrew Bible's vision of liberation from sin that is enacted socially, creating a new sociopolitical order and uniting class divisions across Israel. As Trocmé notes, in addition to ministering to various classes of people (Jews and gentiles, rich and poor, and so on), Christ's ministry ranges across the fortified cities of Galilee, uniting these polities into one body of disciples. The sociopolitical expansion of this peace mirrors the sacramental vision of peace that undergirds Trocmé's vision of who Jesus is and what the church is to be. Accordingly, Christ's commandments are not to be enacted solely by individual followers of Jesus in a series of situations but are to be the enacted life of the church together. Refusing interpretations of the Sermon on the Mount in which the Sermon depicts eschatological reality or purely individualist options, Trocmé argues that the norm of the Old Testament was that of the community. As such, the people of the church are to enact these teachings now, together.[6]

The *goel* of the people, who redeems them through nonviolent love, enacts the kingdom of God in a way that "commits to the redemption of the individual person." The nonviolent church, in turn, is "a matter of showing compassion, of saving and redeeming, of being a healing community." This way, which is participation in the very person of Jesus, is only available as a work of God and not, in distinction from Gandhi's view, as a tactical move toward a political end. The distinction Trocmé makes between the way of Gandhi, as commendable as it is, and the way of Jesus turns on this: participation in the power

6. Trocmé, *Jesus and the Nonviolent Revolution*, 46, 65.

of God available through Jesus Christ, who is the mediator of humanity to God.[7]

Trocmé thus connects the mediation of Christ, the creation of the people of God, and the practice of the Christian community. In doing so, Trocmé takes a different path than nineteenth-century liberal theology—and a different path than the way that the nonviolent community will be appropriated by many in the twentieth century. For in much nineteenth-century liberal theology, dogmatic claims about the nature of God are available to us through moral behaviors: to know God is to love people. While in Scripture, the knowledge of God and the love that the Christian has for others are connected, for liberals in the nineteenth century, one knows *who* God is *as* one enacts moral behaviors. The substance of God is transposed into a moral axiom.

This is not to say that the twentieth century—in emphasizing the practical nature of the Christian faith or the imitation of Christ—is simply repeating the nineteenth century's mantras. But across the modern era, as Christians continued to sort out the relationship between the church and the peace that is God, two roads began to emerge: (1) that the peace of God manifests itself *as the church's liturgical gathering* and (2) that the peace of God manifests itself through *the actions and witness* of the church. This is in some ways an artificial separation, as most theologians will affirm both to some degree. But the question appears in terms of whether what is happening is an *embodiment* of God's peace or an *imitation* of God's peace. In his work, Trocmé holds together what will sometimes come apart.

7. Trocmé, *Jesus and the Nonviolent Revolution*, 145, 146, 153. Where multiple page numbers appear within a single note at the end of a paragraph, the numbers correspond, in order, to the quotations within that paragraph.

Nonviolence in the Christian Canon

Biblical scholars have expanded Trocmé's thesis beyond the Gospels to the remaining canon of the New Testament and to the precedents of the Hebrew Bible, or the Old Testament. The concern is not simply whether nonviolence is articulated by Jesus for his disciples but also whether Christian nonviolence is thoroughly *canonical*: Does Jesus offer his disciples (and thus the church) something that is continued from the Old Testament to the New Testament? Is this teaching new, or is it already a presumption for Israel as well? What is at stake in these questions is whether Christian nonviolence is consistent with Hebrew Scriptures or whether it entails Christian supersessionism.

In her 1984 text, *My Enemy Is My Guest: Jesus and Violence in Luke*, trailblazing Catholic New Testament scholar J. Massyngbaerde Ford argues that Jesus's nonviolence is indeed a new development from what came before, with John the Baptist as a transitional figure between the old and new.[8] Thus, for Ford, Elizabeth's blessing of Mary in Luke 1 harks back to blessings bestowed on Jael in Judges 5 and on Judith in the Book of Judith 13. Ford writes, "It is interesting that these two women are blessed for a heroic, nationalistic, but violent course of action. In other words they were women zealots, somewhat analogous to Phinehas and Elijah. Mary is praised by Elizabeth in words that would clearly remind Jewish readers of these two women zealots." Likewise, Ford describes Mary's song, the Magnificat (Luke 1:46–55), as bearing "all the marks of a holy-war song."[9]

---

8. Ford was just the second female professor at the University of Notre Dame in South Bend, Indiana, when she was hired there in 1965, and three years later she was the first to receive tenure. See Garvy, "In Memoriam."

9. Ford, *My Enemy Is My Guest*, 19–20.

In John the Baptist's teaching in Luke's Gospel, Ford sees a transition beginning to take place from the violent messianism of Mary and Elizabeth to the nonviolence of Jesus. She observes of John the Baptist's teaching to the crowds, tax collectors, and soldiers that he "checks any violent reaction to their circumstances, but he does not ask either the tax collectors or the soldiers to relinquish their occupations." For Ford, then, the nonviolence of Jesus in the Gospel of Luke is truly something new within the canon. Through his parables and teachings, the Lukan Jesus teaches that "disciples must be ready to carry their cross for the sake of the kingdom." Ford writes that "Jesus' demands of his disciples are as radical as those demanded of persons in military service. He will not exclude [persons with disabilities]. He teaches his followers not to take vengeance but to await God's vindication of their cause, and to pray unceasingly." Ford concludes, "It is surely Luke's intention that all Christians should follow in Jesus' footsteps." As a New Testament scholar utilizing the tools of redaction criticism, Ford is reluctant to claim that the New Testament or even the Gospels consistently present Jesus as teaching and embodying nonviolence. For her, the nonviolent Jesus is "one of the special features of Luke (and John)." At the same time, as a Christian, she believes that Luke's message is addressed to contemporary Western Christians just as much as it is to first-century Christians in Rome. "In the contemporary world, where terrorism, violence, crime, war, and poverty are the most important issues of the day," Ford writes, "this aspect of Luke's Gospel is acutely pertinent."[10]

New Testament scholar Scot McKnight echoes the thesis of Trocmé and Ford in his writings on the Gospels. "The peace Jesus is talking about," writes McKnight, "is redemptive peace: it comes in Christ. As Jesus said . . . , 'In me you may have

10. Ford, *My Enemy Is My Guest*, 41, 105, 107, 137.

peace.' This means the peace he's talking about is *ecclesial* peace. . . . The primary way we influence the world is by summoning the world out of its worldliness into the church, where true peace can be found."[11] Whereas Trocmé and Ford focus primarily on the Gospel of Luke, McKnight demonstrates that the presumption of nonviolence for Christian disciples is present throughout the letters of Paul as well. In the letter to the Romans, McKnight observes, the advocacy for the weak by the strong issues forth not in violent defense but in suffering on their behalf. At the same time, more frequent Pauline themes of suffering, bearing of burdens, and patience become ways of instantiating the theme of enemy-love into the life of the early churches.[12]

New Testament scholar Richard Hays echoes these conclusions, particularly noting that from the perspective of the New Testament, the ethos of Jesus was expected to be that of the community, learned through the disciplines of community life.[13] Instead of leaving this as simply a teaching of Jesus, Hays broaches the canonical question in his reading of Romans 5:8–10: "How does God treat enemies? Rather than killing them, Paul declares, he gives his Son to die for them. This has profound implications for the subsequent behavior of those who are reconciled to God through Jesus's death: to be 'saved by his life' means to enter into a life that recapitulates the pattern of Christ's self-giving. . . . It is evident,

11. McKnight, *Kingdom Conspiracy*, 171.

12. McKnight, *Reading Romans Backwards*, 46–50. For McKnight's own account of nonviolence in the teachings of Jesus, which then become presumptions for communities of disciples, see McKnight, *Sermon on the Mount*, 130–38.

13. Hays, *Moral Vision of the New Testament*, 324: "The suggestion that the teaching of the Sermon is intended only for a special class of supersanctified Christians is discredited by the Great Commission at the conclusion of the Gospel. *All* baptized believers are to be taught to observe *all* that Jesus commanded" (emphasis original).

then, that those whose lives are reshaped in Christ must deal with enemies in the same way that God in Christ dealt with enemies."[14]

In the event that the teachings of Jesus differ from particular Old Testament texts, Hays simply asserts that "the New Testament vision trumps the Old Testament."[15] It is here that the question of church formation comes to the center, for if the church is formed according to the Scriptures, then the presence of this ethic in the Old Testament becomes an acute question. If nonviolence is intrinsic to the Christian life because it is participatory in the redemptive work of the world in Christ, then its *absence* in the Old Testament would raise serious questions, not least of which is whether second-century heretic Marcion was right that the God of the Old Testament and the God of the New Testament are in fact two different gods.

The question of the canonical presence of Jesus's ethic can be dealt with in a variety of ways. Perhaps, like dietary laws, the *herem* (God's command to destroy enemies) was simply a command contingent on a particular era in the divine economy, or perhaps the accounts of violence in the Old Testament were more hyperbolic than historical. Preston Sprinkle offers a different take: while Jesus's nonviolence is clear and binding on New Testament congregations, the Old Testament does not materially deviate from this teaching. Examination of the key Old Testament texts, such as

14. Hays, *Moral Vision of the New Testament*, 330. New Testament scholar Michael Gorman develops this theme of participation in Christ in Paul's letters, which Gorman describes as the disciple "becoming the gospel of peace." See Gorman, *Becoming the Gospel*, especially chapter 5, "Becoming the Gospel of Peace (I)," 142–80, and chapter 6, "Becoming the Gospel of Peace (II)," 181–211. In his tome *Covenant of Peace*, New Testament scholar Willard Swartley argues that peace is a pervasive theme throughout the New Testament. On the role of the disciple in imitating the nonviolent suffering of Christ, see especially chapter 13, "Discipleship and Imitation of Jesus the Suffering Servant," 356–76.

15. Hays, *Moral Vision of the New Testament*, 336.

Deuteronomy 20, indicates a nonmilitaristic kind of warfare that emphasizes divine action rather than military prowess or just war. Likewise, the eschatological vision of Isaiah points toward the practice and person of Christ. Jesus, a Messiah in the spirit of Deuteronomy 17, operates not in violation of the Old Testament but in continuity with it. In this way, Sprinkle contends, transposing Jesus's teaching on violence from the Sermon on the Mount into the communal practice of the early churches (seen not only in Paul's churches but also in the other apostolic writings) creates continuity across the canon of Scripture. A Christian need not pick between Testaments but can freely affirm that the God of Scripture—from beginning to end—calls forth a people who trust not in violence but in God for their lives.[16]

Nonviolence and the Practice of the Church

That Trocmé's thesis is well known, even for those who have never read Trocmé, is due in no small part to Mennonite theologian and ethicist John Howard Yoder's widely read 1972 book, *The Politics of Jesus*, which adopts wholesale many portions of Trocmé's work.[17] Indeed, a side-by-side reading of the two texts demonstrates that many of the ideas of the first seven chapters of Yoder's *Politics of Jesus* follow not only the arguments but also the sequence of arguments laid out in Trocmé's *Jesus and the Nonviolent Revolution*, though Trocmé is only credited with the material appearing in the chapter on Jubilee in particular. Yoder's writing on nonviolence spans nearly fifty years and multiple texts, but on this point it retains great consistency: the church

16. Sprinkle, *Fight*, 58–61, 109–13, 151–215. See also Cramer, "Evangelical Hermeneutics, Anabaptist Ethics."

17. For a fuller treatment of Yoder's nonviolence in relation to ecclesiology, see Werntz, *Bodies of Peace*, 59–106.

bears witness to the lordship of Christ over all creation, which means that the church's witness to nonviolence is to be both embodied and demonstrated by analogy to the world.[18] The world understands the moral commitments of the church, however, through its exercise of "middle axioms," ways of communicating the moral commitments of the church to political life.[19]

The locus for forming a Christian commitment to nonviolence, for Yoder, is the church community. Expanding Trocmé's thesis, Yoder argues for the various ways nonviolence not only marks the nature of imitation of Christ but also is intrinsic to what it means to be able to *identify* God both in the Hebrew Bible and in the New Testament: "When, therefore, Jesus used the language of liberation and revolution, announcing a restoration of 'kingdom' community and a new pattern of life, without predicting or authorizing particular violent techniques for achieving his good ends, he need not have seemed to his listeners to be a dreamer; he could very easily have been understood as updating the faith of Jehoshaphat and Hezekiah, a faith whereby a believing people would be saved despite their weakness, on condition that they 'be still and wait to see the salvation of the Lord.'"[20]

Yoder's identification of nonviolence as not only the way of the church but also the way of the people of God across the

18. For his description of the relationship between church and world, see J. Yoder, "Otherness of the Church."

19. For his description of middle axioms, see J. Yoder, *Christian Witness to the State*, 72–73. Yoder borrows this language from earlier Christian realists and eventually stops using it, preferring instead to speak of the paradigmatic function of Christian practices. See, for example, J. Yoder, *Body Politics*. Still, the function is similar: to translate Christian ethics and practices into language and practices that can be understood and adopted by those who do not profess Christian faith. On the origin of "middle axioms" among Christian realists, Georgia Harkness writes: "J. H. Oldham has coined the phrase 'middle axioms,' and the term is effectively used by John C. Bennett in *Christian Ethics and Social Policy*" (*Christian Ethics*, 190). See chapter 5 below for further discussion of Harkness and middle axioms. For more on Yoder's use of the term, see Cramer, "Realistic Transformation," 503–6.

20. J. Yoder, *Politics of Jesus*, 84.

testaments is a striking addition to Trocmé. But it also emphasizes that being the people of God means being nonviolent, for it is in this particular way of existence in the world that we know the presence of God. The structure of *Politics of Jesus* in particular connects faithfulness in the days of Israel, life in the apostolic church, and even the eschatological return of Christ with this mode of nonviolence present in the teachings and life of Jesus. The refusal of violence in the eschatological return of Christ, together with treating the holy wars of the Old Testament as "legend," creates a strong link between a nonviolent people of God and the knowledge of the God of Israel and Jesus.[21] This nonviolence, which is intrinsic to God's presence to creation, is cultivated then by the church in a variety of practices, including its use of polity as communal reasoning rather than as an exercise of power and its use of ecumenical dialogue as conversation rather than as "Constantinian" force.[22]

The emphasis on the habituation of the church opens up the notion that to be nonviolent is a matter of being habituated by the presence of God. But Yoder goes further by making this presence of God—namely, the habit of nonviolence—into one of the defining features of the church's internal life and external witness. Whereas New Testament scholars like Sprinkle, for example, see Jesus's nonviolence as consistent with the Old Testament, Yoder goes beyond this by suggesting that nonviolence is intrinsic to God's own presence. In other words, nonviolence is simply what God is like and thus what the church must be in order to have a witness in the world.[23]

21. J. Yoder, *Politics of Jesus*, 228–30, 86.
22. For these examples, see J. Yoder, "Hermeneutics of Peoplehood," and J. Yoder, "Nature of the Unity We Seek."
23. For a practical application of this approach by one of Yoder's students, see Camp, *Mere Discipleship*, especially chapter 7, "Worship: Why Disciples Love Their Enemies," 129–47.

Gerald Mast and J. Denny Weaver, in *Defenseless Christianity: Anabaptism for a Nonviolent Church*, continue Yoder's trajectory, building out edges of the relationship between church and nonviolence that are not immediately obvious in Yoder. For Yoder, nonviolence is the most obvious way of naming the "style" of faith appropriate for Christians, embodied not only in one's commitments concerning war but also in how one approaches church life.[24] But for Mast and Weaver, the *act* of nonviolence comes to the forefront as a defining dogmatic commitment of the church: "If the particular story of Jesus is a norm that gives the church its distinct character and shapes its communal practices, then peacemaking and the *rejection of violence* are incipient as the privileged manifestation of discipleship or of following the example of Jesus. . . . Since rejection of violence is intrinsic to the story and work of Jesus, we do not separate it from our confession of Jesus as Lord and norm."[25]

With this practice as a central norm, then, the church's "defenselessness" becomes more apparent, with other elements of church polity ordered by this conviction. Separation from the world, a key New Testament motif, becomes a way to distance oneself from systemic violence while not being antagonistic, for example. Likewise, the Lord's Supper is an occasion for learning how to be a servant leader, to give of oneself and live sacrificially. These practices of service and sacrifice may very well be entailed by a life of discipleship, but the difference between Yoder, on the one hand, and Mast and Weaver, on the other, is the loss of the middle axiom, that translation point that allows the commitments of the church to transcend their ethical meaning alone.[26]

24. See, however, our discussion of Yoder's betrayal of his nonviolent ethic in the preface to this book and the conclusion to this chapter.

25. Mast and Weaver, *Defenseless Christianity*, 76, emphasis original.

26. Mast and Weaver, *Defenseless Christianity*, 82, 88–89.

These thinkers raise important questions about what it means for the formation that occurs in the church to contribute to the work of nonviolence. With Yoder to a lesser degree, and more directly in Mast and Weaver, we find the question of how a commitment to living defenselessly sits among other Christian convictions. Does it determine the shape of other commitments? For example, does baptism mean, as Mast and Weaver contend, being able to recognize the value of all life? Or, more directly, can one call oneself a disciple of Jesus if one does not take nonviolence to be an absolute value?[27]

In his criticism of Yoder, just war thinker Nigel Biggar contends that packaging together the person of Jesus with the value of nonviolence conflates fidelity to Jesus (the second person of the Trinity) with the ethic of the disciples: to be responsive to God, one must not reject responsibility to God's world. As such, one can be a soldier and a Christian, as Jesus's disciples are called to be responsible not only to God but also to the history in which they live: to adopt nonviolence as inseparable from commitment to God is ultimately to be a bad disciple.[28] While those committed to Christian nonviolence will no doubt disagree with Biggar on many things, he troubles the association of church with nonviolence by raising an important question: Can a church body commit to nonviolence *without* it being as central to the church's identity as Mast and Weaver suggest?

Exceptions to Nonviolence for Christian Discipleship?

Dietrich Bonhoeffer offers one possible way forward—but not without some complications. Bonhoeffer, a German theologian and pastor living under the Nazi regime, enjoys a kind of exotic

---

27. Mast and Weaver, *Defenseless Christianity*, 86.
28. Biggar, *In Defence of War*, 31–34.

reputation due to lack of clarity about his role in an assassination attempt on Adolf Hitler.[29] On the one hand, Bonhoeffer was indisputably involved in the political resistance to the Third Reich. On the other hand, Bonhoeffer writes in his famous *Discipleship* that "Jesus' followers are called to peace. When Jesus called them they found peace. Jesus is their peace. Now they are not only to have peace, but they are to make peace. To do this they renounce violence and strife. . . . Jesus' disciples maintain peace by choosing to suffer instead of causing others to suffer."[30]

Critical to understanding Bonhoeffer is appreciating his emphasis—particularly when thinking about the role of the Christian in a world of violence—that the Christian always proceeds *as a Christian* in the world. Christians work as those who are flung out into the world until such a time as they gather together with the body of Christ again, and their ethics in the world are always conditioned by seeing Christ (and thus, the body of Christ) as the key to the world's preservation.[31]

This is different than saying that everything that the Christian does is restricted by the *key* in which it would happen in church. In the church, we are gathered in baptism and communion; as such, what we do in church is analogous to what we do in the world, but the ethic of Jesus is the *way* by which we are formed. While we are joined with the first hearers of Jesus, we are joined to them and to Jesus in *our* day, as the church in *our* place: "The problem of following Christ shows itself here to be a hermeneutical problem. But it should be clear to a Gospel-oriented hermeneutic that we cannot simply identify ourselves directly with those called by Jesus. . . . Simple obedience would be misunderstood hermeneutically if we were to act and follow

---

29. For the details of the controversy, see Nation, Siegrist, and Umbel, *Bonhoeffer the Assassin?*

30. Bonhoeffer, *Discipleship*, 108.

31. See Bonhoeffer, *Life Together*, 83–95.

as if we were contemporaries of the biblical disciples. But the Christ proclaimed to us in scripture is, through every word he says, the one whose gift of faith is granted only to the obedient, faith to the obedient alone."[32]

This does not mean—contrary to some accounts that make Bonhoeffer into a Niebuhrian realist who abandons his ethic in the face of the hard facts of the world—that the disciple takes the peace of Christ as a "principle" to be enacted by any means necessary. Rather, it means that the way of enacting the life of Jesus is not up to the disciples to choose; disciples are bound to Jesus, not to the ethic of nonviolence.

Bonhoeffer always wrote through the lens of being the "church-community," anticipating that the command to the church will be made concrete in some way by God. The way of the church in the wider scope of creation means that the church is always being formed in discipleship. In the case of peacemaking, disciples try to act in ways that are faithful to the witness and person of Jesus but not as those who slavishly repeat the actions of Jesus. In other words, Bonhoeffer rejects both a just war framework that makes Jesus's nonviolence a matter of interpersonal relations or an eschatological ideal and an absolutist pacifist framework that would not make use of the state in order to enact the call of Christ. The church will enact peace in a way consistent with Jesus and specifically will seek to bring people into the heart of that peace—the presence of Christ in worship—but the way it will do this consistently is not for the church to determine in advance. This is not to say that the church has an option as to whether to offer its witness but simply that social issues—particularly how and when to engage them—are considered according to how disciples can reestablish the conditions of life that the body of Christ shares with all creation. In responding to the wounds of

32. Bonhoeffer, *Discipleship*, 82.

creation, disciples follow Christ's call, formed as members of the church but not bound absolutely to one ethical rendering of the way of Jesus.[33]

Catholic theologian and ethicist Gerald Schlabach echoes this vision. For Schlabach, the church is to be the sacrament for the world, a pilgrim people that binds together the world in peace but not because it first and foremost sends an ethic of nonviolence into the world. Because the church is catholic—that is, a universal body that encompasses all differences and traverses all social divisions—the church is quite literally the body that holds together the divisions of creation in itself. The church is a kind of nesting doll within societies, "communities embedded within communities, people embedded within peoples." A church formed by the peace of Christ fills the surrounding society with that peace by its very existence, which removes division across class, gender, and race. Disciples formed by the Sermon on the Mount are willing to break the rule of retaliation and revenge in order to transform the world's violence. Schlabach, like Bonhoeffer, sees the call of Christians not as one of repetition of a principle such as "nonresistance" or "effectiveness." Rather, Christians are to be formed according to the Beatitudes of the Sermon on the Mount, which culminate in the love of enemies.[34]

Discipleship, Church, and Nonviolence

The distinction between the two approaches to nonviolence of Christian discipleship that we have discussed—one that began with Trocmé and one that was represented by Bonhoeffer—may

33. DeJonge, *Bonhoeffer on Resistance*, 84, 155. Ultimately, as Bonhoeffer says in *Ethics*, 268, those who "act responsibly (i.e., according to the call of Christ into the world) place their action into the hands of God and live by God's grace and judgment."

34. Schlabach, *Pilgrim People*, 189, 193, 259. For a moving memoir on learning to love enemies, see Wells and Owen, *Living without Enemies*.

seem to be a matter of hairsplitting. After all, both hold that nonviolence is tied to the work of Christian formation, and both hold that the work of Christian churches is to train people to be faithful followers of Christ.[35] But where the two diverge is on how tightly to hold to nonviolence as a core principle of what it means to be the church. As we saw with Trocmé, the incarnation of Christ issues forth in a body, the church, which follows the way of Jesus throughout the entire world: the argument is about what it means to embody that peace.

In the work of Mast and Weaver, nonviolence is inextricable from the person of Jesus, to the degree that, from first to last, being a Christian entails a commitment to nonviolence. This is not, in some ways, dissimilar from Bonhoeffer and Schlabach, for whom being the people of Christ means being peacemakers. But for Bonhoeffer and Schlabach, being the people of Jesus means that nonviolence emerges as the action of what the church is, not as its core commitment without which it ceases to be the church.

By tying Jesus and nonviolence so firmly together, Mast and Weaver create a situation wherein Christians who engage in violence for any reason find themselves not just disobedient but *heretics*—those who have offered the world a different Jesus. By the same token, Bonhoeffer and Schlabach, in taking the sacramental approach that confesses that Christ envelops the world prior to our actions, run the risk of opening a gap between being Christian and holding to the ethic of Jesus with respect to violence. The two paths unite in this: being a Christian means being formed in discipleship as a member of the body of Christ who acts together with the body of Christ to be

35. For a discussion of the contrasting approaches to resisting the Nazis by Bonhoeffer and the Confessing Church, on the one hand, and by Trocmé and the community of Le Chambon, on the other, see Harvey, *Taking Hold of the Real*, chapter 9, "Tale of Two Pastors," 269–301.

a witness to the world. The fractures of violence run deep in the world, and, ultimately, only a people formed in the image of Christ's wisdom can know what it means to be peacemakers when that act is called forth from them.

Conclusion

In the end, nonviolence of Christian discipleship binds the disciple to a way not of their choosing. In discussions surrounding the virtue or the feasibility of Christian nonviolence, Oliver O'Donovan has argued that Christian nonviolence therefore represents a refusal to engage in making judgments within time.[36] What O'Donovan neglects in this assessment, however, is that Christian nonviolence is not abandoning making all judgments. Rather, if Christ is the Lord of creation, the one who commands his disciples to live nonviolently, being a disciple will entail not making use of all paths that might present themselves within creation. By emphasizing habituation, communities of formation, and discipleship, this mode of nonviolence trades on being a witness to the nations, living within violence and providing shelter within it without becoming like it.

Nevertheless, of all the streams of Christian nonviolence discussed in this book, nonviolence of Christian discipleship is the one most in need of further archeological retrieval and critical scrutiny. In the twentieth century, there was perhaps no Christian—with the exception of Martin Luther King Jr., whom we discuss in chapter 6—more associated with Christian nonviolence than John Howard Yoder. His work both popularized and expanded interest in Christian nonviolence. But with his rise in popularity, other voices we have highlighted in this chapter were eclipsed. Moreover, while the debts owed to his

36. O'Donovan, *Just War Revisited*, 7–8.

scholarship are significant, his popularity allowed him cover for sexual violence in his own life.[37] It is for this reason that we cannot ignore his influence but must critically scrutinize it. While we acknowledge his contribution to this form of Christian nonviolence, we have also shown that his contribution was not singular but was one voice in a larger chorus. As we evaluate nonviolence of Christian discipleship in light of his influence, we also seek to explore other streams of Christian nonviolence that are not as indebted to his writing.

37. On Yoder's history of sexual violence and its relation to his theological ethics, see Cramer et al., "Theology and Misconduct"; Goossen, "'Defanging the Beast'"; Villegas, "Ecclesial Ethics of John Howard Yoder's Abuse."

Nonviolence as Christian Virtue

BECOMING A PEACEABLE PEOPLE

I n his devastating essay "How to Tell a True War Story," author Tim O'Brien writes,

> A true war story is never moral. It does not instruct, nor encourage virtue, nor suggest models of proper human behavior, nor restrain men from doing the things men have always done. If a story seems moral, do not believe it. If at the end of a war story you feel uplifted, or if you feel that some small bit of rectitude has been salvaged from the larger waste, then you have been made the victim of a very old and terrible lie. There is no rectitude whatsoever. There is no virtue. As a first rule of thumb, therefore, you can tell a true war story by its absolute and uncompromising allegiance to obscenity and evil.[1]

O'Brien's bleak depiction of war questions the claim that participating in war is both a virtuous thing to do and something

1. T. O'Brien, *Things They Carried*, 68–69.

that makes a person virtuous. Centuries of war literature have
been devoted to this theme, and so, for O'Brien—a Vietnam
War veteran—to claim that war is morally deformative raises
serious questions: Is there a place for virtue—for human flourishing in goodness—in the midst of conflict? Do discussions
of virtue matter when lives are at stake?

The word *virtue*, when used here, does not mean the same
thing as piety but instead conveys a comprehensive vision
of what it means to be fully human before God. The virtues
prompt us to wrestle with this fundamental question: *What is
the end toward which humans are meant to live?* A virtuous
person is one whose desires, heart, aspirations, and actions are
directed toward God, their true end.[2] Thus the issue O'Brien
and centuries of writers before him have wrestled with is the
relationship between violence and fully flourishing as God's
creatures.

Virtue arguments work in a different way than other kinds
of arguments against war. They require us first to examine
what is meant by the virtues themselves. Whereas arguments
for nonviolence rooted in an encounter with God, national
self-interest, or political vision seem straightforward, appealing
to nonviolence on the basis of virtue can seem evasive. Why
be concerned with questions of virtue when life and death are
on the line? The answer is this: because war is a human activity, we cannot put aside what it means to be good and human
when violence arises but must continue to pursue the good,
particularly in times of conflict.

When the issue of virtue is raised in discussions of Christianity and violence, the most common connection is to just

2. For two accessible introductions to the nature of the virtues in the Christian
life, see Wadell, *Happiness and the Christian Life*; Meilaender, *Theory and Practice
of Virtue*.

war. In the writings of the fourth-century theologian Augustine, we find the admonition to fight such that peace, and not
violence, is the object of our desire. Augustine admonishes
the Christian that you must, "even in waging war, cherish the
spirit of a peacemaker, that, by conquering those whom you
attack, you may lead them back to the advantages of peace."[3]
War, for Augustine, could be undertaken, provided that it was
aiming toward obedience to God and done with the proper
set of virtues and dispositions. There were dissenters to this
compatibility of war and Christian virtue, but Augustine's
vision—though developed and modified—continued for many
centuries. Over time, just war theory became detached from
a specifically Christian context and became the language of
statecraft, with the virtues becoming a less-considered aspect
of whether and how Christians should engage in violence.[4]

Recent Christian just war proponents have attempted to re-
vive the older conception—that Christians need the virtues for,
among other things, participating in conflict well.[5] Yet, in this
chapter, we describe an alternate stream of Christian thought
that identifies nonviolence among the Christian virtues and
therefore argues that the virtuous Christian person is one who
refuses to participate in violence—even on behalf of a war
that might fit the traditional just war criteria. To describe this
stream of Christian nonviolence, we draw on the works of a
number of Catholic theologians, activists, and peace studies
scholars—Dorothy Day, Leonardo Boff, Lisa Sowle Cahill, Eli
McCarthy, Pope Francis, and others—as well as prominent

3. Augustine, *Letter 189* (to Boniface), quoted in Holmes, *War and Christian
Ethics*, 62–63.
4. Just war considerations also preceded its Christian context, as the writings of
Roman statesman Cicero (106–43 BC) influenced Augustine's own considerations
of the justice of war.
5. Bell, *Just War as Christian Discipleship*. See also Stassen, "Holistic, Interactive
Character Formation for Just Peacemaking," 3–28.

Protestant theological ethicist Stanley Hauerwas, and other virtue ethicists. First, though, we turn to the thought of the great medieval theologian and developer of both just war and virtue theory, Thomas Aquinas, for his account of the virtues and their role in the Christian life.

Natural and Supernatural Virtues

Virtue is participation in goodness in the deepest possible sense. More than simply being nice, virtue names what is most true about the ordering of human life and what is most true about the nature of creation itself. Thus, virtue theory is not about what works but about what is most appropriate for all that God has created. Being virtuous is not immediate but is acquired as a person's life is retrained by God's work. Accordingly, being virtuous involves not only interior dispositions but also skills and habits. This is not the same as mastering a technique—as if being virtuous were a set of instructions—but is more akin to acquiring a habit or skill that "permits [one] to respond creatively to new situations or unanticipated difficulties."[6] Or, as Bernard Haring, a Catholic Redemptorist priest and leading light in twentieth-century Catholic biblical ethics, has described it, to be virtuous is to have all of our moral sensibilities sanctified at the roots by God's grace, such that all that we do reflects God's intent for creation.[7]

The virtues are traditionally described in two categories—the natural and the supernatural, or the acquired and the infused. But because, as Haring suggests, grace "sanctifies the very root and source of these acts," being virtuous involves not simply being a moral person (the natural virtues) but also

6. Meilaender, *Theory and Practice of Virtue*, 9.
7. Haring, *Law of Christ*, 491–96.

allowing those natural habits of being a moral human to be completed by the supernatural virtues of faith, hope, and love. This is not to say that people other than Christians cannot be moral; the natural virtues are present in a variety of persons. But there is a sense in which the natural acquired virtues, apart from the supernatural infused virtues (given by supernatural grace), remain incomplete. In other words, the Christian cannot be just without further considering what it means for them to be a just *Christian*, and cannot be courageous without having that image filtered through the person of Christ, the true vision of faith, hope, and love.

For medieval theologian Thomas Aquinas—whose work is at the root of much modern Christian thinking about the nature of virtue—the natural virtues and the supernatural virtues relate to and inform one another but are not the same.[8] Broadly speaking, for Thomas, the natural virtues are in need of completion by the theological ones. This is more than simply a hermeneutical move. It is not that the virtues of courage and fortitude *look* different for Christians; rather, it is that, by God's grace, they are made more than they were, transfigured and raised up.

Thomas provides the best example of how these two forms of virtue converge and diverge. In his *Summa Theologica*, Thomas points to the martyr as the highest example of virtue when considering what the nature of fortitude (or courage) consists of—for martyrdom is done with God in view, is done in the imitation of Christ, and "is the most perfect of human acts in respect of its genus, as being the sign of the greatest charity."[9]

8. How to best interpret this relationship has a long history that will not be rehearsed here. For an overview, see Porter, "Virtue," in Meilaender and Werpehowski, *Oxford Handbook of Theological Ethics*, 205–20.

9. Thomas Aquinas, *Summa Theologica* II-II.124.3, s.c. See Clark, "Is Martyrdom Virtuous?"; Hauerwas and Pinches, *Christians among the Virtues*, 149–65.

For Thomas, death in conformity to Christ eclipses other forms of courage, such as that of the solider, who is the exemplar of natural courage. The virtuous solider—one who exemplifies proper courage, justice, prudence, and temperance—is ranked lower by Thomas than the martyr because martyrs lose their life in imitation of Christ. In doing so, martyrs display the fullest example of what virtue is: a life fully formed toward God. For Thomas, many soldiers exhibit courage, act justly, and behave temperately and with wisdom. But martyrs, who do all these things in the imitation of Christ, direct their death not toward preserving the state or protecting their neighbor but toward God in faith, hope, and love.

The relationship between the natural virtues and the super-natural ones—the way in which faith, hope, and love reframe and reorder how we think about living moral lives—becomes significant for virtue arguments for Christian nonviolence in two ways. First, Christian nonviolence (as imitation of Jesus) becomes a practice by which we are formed into the image of Christ. Not only are nonviolent Christians trained to be virtu-ous people—courageous in the face of danger, for example—but through habits of nonviolence, their natural passions and desires are refocused toward Christ. Second, if action is what displays the full range of the virtues, then Christian nonvio-lence shows the world what it means to be fully human.

Nonviolence as the Way of Virtue

With the above brief description of virtue in place, we can now look at a variety of ways in which virtue arguments have laid the groundwork for Christian nonviolence. For some of these, the virtues are best exemplified by the act of Christian nonvio-lence. For others, becoming a virtuous person is inextricable from the practice of nonviolence. What is at stake strikes deep at the question of what it means to live as a Christian—namely, whether one can be mature in the Christian faith as a person whose life is shaped by faith, hope, and love apart from the practice of nonviolence. Thus, when appeals to virtue are made in arguments for nonviolence, more is at stake than saying that nonviolence is an expedient thing. Rather, nonviolence, consistent with Christian virtue, is moral because it coheres with the deep logic of how God has created the world to be and who God has created people to be.

Haring deviates from some interpreters on the virtues. Whereas many interpreters hold to two sets of virtues, the natural and the supernatural,[10] Haring proposes that there is ultimately only one kind of virtue. If what is good is understood by way of Christ, the virtues have to be understood by way of the Beatitudes. Accordingly, if justice is not mediated through God's forgiveness, or if courage is not tempered by notions of loving sacrifice, it is not truly the virtue of God.[11] In this way, for Haring, nonviolence in the manner of the Sermon on the Mount is one of the actions that exemplifies the virtue toward which all Christians are called.[12]

Some proponents of nonviolence as Christian virtue describe virtue as a person's *character* rather than a list of discrete characteristics. For example, Eli McCarthy, in examining what role virtue has to play in peacemaking, points not only to faith, hope, and love but also to compassion, humility, solidarity, and kindness, among others.[13] The virtuous community of peacemakers is always embedded within society such that

10. Some, such as Jean Porter, hold to a reading of Thomas that allows for an intermediary form of virtue between the two. See Porter, "Virtue."

11. Haring, *Christian Renewal in a Changing World*, 20–32.

12. See Gorman, *Inhabiting the Cruciform God*, for a contemporary treatment of the relationship between nonviolence and virtue in the Pauline epistles.

13. McCarthy, *Becoming Nonviolent Peacemakers*, 88–94.

virtue cannot be worked out simply as a matter of the soul but must also include how one lives and makes peace within one's world. The infused virtues (faith, hope, and love) and the natural virtues are inseparable in Christian peacemaking such that one cannot help but take seriously the virtues of Jesus in one's life in the world. McCarthy develops a variety of public policy proposals not as an implication of the virtues but as a way of extending their reach into the world. If the virtues are ultimately indicative of the way God intends the world to be, then the virtues do not have to be translated into policy so much as they have to be articulated as consistent modes of action— that is, as laws. McCarthy is indebted to the work of Haring, who similarly proposes that true virtue—taking root in the soul—coheres to the logic of how God's creation is ordered. In his book on nonviolence, Haring builds on his earlier work on the virtues to suggest that the biblical language of *shalom* bears this out precisely: the virtues are not simply for private perfection but describe what it means for humans to be cohered to the world God has made.[14]

Central to discussions of virtue—particularly as virtue manifests itself in public—is what shape the virtues should take. Typically, *justice* is described as the virtue that binds and shapes the natural virtues, but in Ellen Ott Marshall's work, a nonviolence formed by *love* is the way the virtues allow Christians to engage in public life well.[15] In her work on Christian engagements in public, love begets the practice of moral ambiguity, which in turn leads to a humble posture in public engagements. In this way, nonviolence becomes a style of engaging the world: love takes the shape of nonviolence, embodied in this style of engagement appropriate to public life. As with McCarthy,

14. Haring, *Healing Power of Peace and Nonviolence.*
15. Marshall, *Christians in the Public Square.* For a legal exploration of this theme, see McCarty, "Nonviolent Law?"

the virtues for Marshall operate not in a two-tiered fashion, whereby our normal ways of living out virtue are perfected, but rather in such a way that our life before God and our life in the world are caught up and transfigured together.

This approach to the virtues—leading with love as opposed to one of the natural practices—is precisely the kind of proposal that has come under criticism by just war thinkers and realists, who dismiss it as unrealistic or sentimental. But these kind of realist arguments do not quite address what the virtue arguments have at stake. As we have seen, virtue arguments acknowledge that the violence of the world is not always solved by nonviolence. Rather, the heart of Marshall's proposal—that nonviolence should be the public form of the virtues—pushes critics of nonviolence to recall that nonviolence also requires suffering. It is in suffering, as the apostle Paul writes, that our character is formed more fully into the image of Christ. From the perspective of virtue, it may be that nonviolence—in addition to sometimes "working"—also forms us more truly into Christ's image through suffering for the sake of others.

Becoming Virtuous through a Life of Nonviolence

Dorothy Day, a Marxist convert to Catholicism, often wrote affectionately about her Marxist past, for the things she appreciated about Marxism were the very things she saw brought to fullness in Christianity.[16] Marxists spoke of loving the poor, while Christianity spoke of this *and* of loving their oppressors. Marxists spoke of feeding the poor, while Christianity spoke of this *and* of feeding the soul. For Day, Marxism in many ways represented a glittering vision of temporal life, but Christianity offered that world crowned by the love of God. Throughout her

16. Day, *From Union Square to Rome.*

life, Day thus continued to affirm the natural virtues as she saw them exercised in the most unlikely places, from Ho Chi Minh to Mohandas Gandhi to Cardinal Spellman.[17] And throughout her life, she continued to work in coalitions with Catholics and non-Catholics, seeing the virtuous non-Christian as on the way to the kingdom of God.

Nowhere was Day's approach clearer than with respect to the practice of nonviolence. For Day, if the body of Christ is best described as the unity of God with humanity, then nonviolence—enacting peace in the world—is one of the practices that makes that peace known.[18] War forms us, she said, in all the wrong kinds of virtues. War produces new divisions within humanity and justifies practices that reinforce those divisions in all kinds of normal ways: taxation, nationalist rhetoric, racism, and so forth. Not only does nonviolence bear witness to a completely different way of viewing the world, but practicing it forms us toward God's kingdom by forming in us a wholly different set of virtues.[19] Whereas acts of justice and courage could be seen in many places, nonviolence transfigures these acts by redirecting them toward Christ. Day describes the practice of nonviolence as among the works of mercy, through which people not only witness to Christ's work but also are transformed as they do it.[20]

Robert Brimlow likewise points to how love of God and love of neighbor, while distinct, are interrelated: "Our response to the evildoers we see and fear in our communities is to be one of love, forgiveness, and comfort. . . . The answer to the Hitler question cannot come from the armchair theoreticians of the

---

17. For a full account of Day's nonviolence, see Werntz, *Bodies of Peace*, 107–55.

18. All forms of violence are, for Day, the opposite of the peace made known in the body of Christ. See Day, *Houses of Hospitality*, 148–49.

19. Day, "Fight Conscription." This essay and other *Catholic Worker* letters by Day are accessible at https://www.catholicworker.org/dorothyday.

20. Werntz, *Bodies of Peace*, 144–50.

geopolitical. It is only through prayer and our daily practices that we allow ourselves to be formed into disciples of the Lord and his peacemakers."[21]

Just war advocate Daniel M. Bell Jr. pushes back at this point, arguing that trusting in God's grace, exercising love of the innocent, and hoping in God's provision do not entail Christian nonviolence; rather, for Bell, to be formed in faith, hope, and love means a commitment to justified war when needed.[22] Bell and proponents of nonviolence as Christian virtue diverge on the question of whether the virtues embodied in the life of Jesus are the same virtues that should be practiced by Christians today. Day, for example, would agree that soldiers exhibit courage and that sometimes governments make just determinations, but she would insist that such virtues are not the same as the fullness of virtue seen in the person of Jesus.

As Lisa Sowle Cahill argues, a commitment to nonviolence as Christian virtue is not necessarily at odds with a realist perspective on conflict but can augment the findings of nonviolent realists.[23] If Jesus is the culmination of what it means to be a creature of God, then the moral approach of Jesus can come to bear on the logic of the natural world as well. In her survey of Christian teaching on war and peace, Cahill points out how Christian pacifism is "nourished primarily in spiritual fellowship, prayer, and communal rededication to social action," in contrast to just war theory.[24] Built on how nonviolence coheres to the heart of the natural law, the flexibility of nonviolence coheres to the manifold ways humans live by appealing to reason, prudence, Scripture, and

21. Brimlow, *What about Hitler?*, 189–90.

22. Bell, *Just War as Christian Discipleship*, 240–42. Similar claims are extended in Capizzi, *Politics, Justice and War*.

23. Cahill, "Church for Peace."

24. Cahill, *Love Your Enemies*, 235. As McCarthy observes in *Nonviolent Peacemakers*, for Cahill, nonviolence is about conversion (84).

the life of the virtues.[25] The life of nonviolence, though find-
ing application in politics, begins *not* with politics but in the
formation of virtue.

Forming the Virtue of Nonviolence in the Church

Since the late 1970s, Stanley Hauerwas has been at the forefront of the recovery of virtue among Protestant Christian ethics, albeit in an idiosyncratic way. Rather than beginning by
enumerating the virtues as Thomas does, Hauerwas speaks of
character as the all-encompassing form of human life.[26] If we
take our cues from the person of Jesus as to what a virtuous
life looks like, Hauerwas contends, the picture of virtue is inseparable from being a person of nonviolence. We learn how
to be this kind of person not by following axioms or rules but
by being conformed to the character of Jesus in the community
of the church.[27]

Nonviolence, as one of the practices we learn in church, becomes habitual over time, interwoven with how we understand
the classical virtues. For example, in his published letters to
his godson, Hauerwas interweaves descriptions of the virtues
with their nonviolent character, as seen in his discussions of
hope, patience, friendship, and justice.[28] For Hauerwas, being
nonviolent is not a natural virtue but one that is made possible by grace as we inhabit the life of the church. This being
said, once we become virtuous people, we begin to see nonviolence as intrinsic to the logic of creation itself: "An eschatological account of creation does not necessarily commit one

25. Cahill, *Love Your Enemies*, 236.
26. Hauerwas, *Character and the Christian Life*.
27. See Hauerwas, *Peaceable Kingdom*, 83–92; Hauerwas, *Community of Character*, 111–54.
28. Hauerwas, *Character of Virtue*, 87–117.

to nonviolence, but it at least puts one in that ballpark. It does so because creation was, after all, God's determinative act of peace. If, therefore, the end is in the beginning, at the very least Christians who justify the Christian participation in war bear the burden of proof."[29]

For Hauerwas, we can only make such a claim about the nature of creation as we become people formed in the image of Christ in the company of Christ's people, the church. Nonviolence is not, in contrast to the realists' perspective, evaluated on policy merits; rather, it is learned inside the Christian community. "The intelligibility of Christian faith," Hauerwas writes, "springs not from independently formulated criteria, but from compelling renditions, faithful performances."[30] The narrative of what it means to be a Christian—including the nonviolence intrinsic to it—is not learned by evaluating nonviolence against secular accounts of the virtuous life; rather, nonviolence is judged according to whether it coheres to Jesus's own life. Hauerwas's account of the virtues is thus interwoven with nonviolence: to be a person of *Christian* virtue is inextricably to be a nonviolent person. For Hauerwas, virtue takes a specific narrative form, embodied in the life of the church, as the church learns to live out the narrative of Scripture in its own day and time.

While agreeing that Christian virtue involves nonviolence, some Catholic thinkers have questioned whether the exclusive attention on the church as the place for learning the virtue of nonviolence is sufficient. Since the 1960s, various Catholic encyclicals and ecclesiastical documents have commended nonviolence as a faithful Christian approach to war.[31] Particularly, they

29. Hauerwas, *Approaching the End*, 21.
30. Hauerwas, *Performing the Faith*, 78.
31. John XXIII, *Pacem in Terris* (1963), §§79–80; Paul IV, *Gaudium et spes* (1965), §§78–82; the National [US] Conference of Catholic Bishops, *Challenge of Peace* (1983) and "Harvest of Justice Is Sown in Peace" (1993); Benedict XVI, "Fighting Poverty

have emphasized, in the words of Pope Francis, "nonviolence as a style of politics for peace." Coupling practices of peacemaking with virtues of the Beatitudes, Francis argues, demonstrates that "active nonviolence is a way of showing that unity is truly more powerful and more fruitful than conflict." For Francis, in contrast to Hauerwas, this upbuilding—this training in virtue—begins in the family; in this way, the virtues of the church spill out into the whole of society. Nonviolence is not simply a performative work of well-formed congregations but also the labor of families; in locating the formative work of nonviolence in families, we can attend to the hidden violences that occur among families in addition to the more public violence of war.[32]

Leonardo Boff likewise locates the work of the virtues outside the church, but for him this work is located within a cosmic frame. He sees all reality—from environmental forces to the dynamics of the human soul—as draped in violence; as such, the virtues of hospitality and peaceableness cannot be limited to the church or even to one religious tradition.[33] The virtues, he writes, must be cosmically located, put into action at every level. Preeminent among the virtues is hospitality, meaning that virtue can only be worked out in the widest possible frame; to work out the virtuous life in a small frame is to exclude others and, thus, to perpetuate violence. For Hauerwas, the question is whether peace can be learned in any meaningful or concrete way if there is no limit to community, for it is in community that we learn in concrete fashion the way of peace and what nonviolence even means. For Boff, in contrast, the peaceable life is one

---

to Build Peace" (2009) and "If You Want to Cultivate Peace" (2010); and Francis, *Angelus* (2013) and "Nonviolence" (2017).

32. Francis, "Nonviolence," §§1, 6, 5. On the disproportionate burden of women for cultivating nonviolence in families, see Gandolfo, "Motherhood, Violence, and Peacemaking." See also chapter 8 below on interpersonal violence and Christian forms of resistance to it.

33. Boff, *Virtues for Another Possible World*, 257–64.

that can only be worked out in interreligious fashion, even at the risk of leaving intelligibly Christian forms of peace behind.

Conclusion

Many just war arguments, both modern and ancient, have coupled participating in war with being virtuous, as war involves courage, the defense of the innocent, and love of one's country. Christian arguments for nonviolence rooted in the virtues do not negate any of these virtues—to defend the innocent is not a bad thing, for example. What is challenged, however, is whether the Christian virtues are compatible with the use of violence.

For the figures in this chapter, becoming a person of virtue is inseparable from enacting nonviolence, though the figures we have discussed differ on precisely what this enactment involves. For some, such as Francis, nonviolence involves dealing with how families relate to one another; for others, such as Day, nonviolence involves both domestic issues and large-scale demonstrations; for still others, such as Hauerwas, the virtue of nonviolence is primarily learned and practiced within the household of the church. But what unites these figures is the perspective that by practicing nonviolence not only do we become people of virtue but our lives also become an argument for Christian nonviolence.

Virtue is a habitual way of being that encompasses all of our actions, whether we are actively protesting war or not. Nonviolence as virtue becomes part of how we live our lives so that being opposed to war is a natural extension of what it means to be a person of virtue in normal circumstances. As Hauerwas puts it, nonviolence—if practiced as a way of life—shows us how frequently we resort to violence in our daily lives and not just in times of war.[34]

34. Hauerwas, *Sanctify Them in the Truth*, 178n2.

Nonviolence of Christian Mysticism

UNITING WITH THE GOD OF PEACE

In his work on peace and the Christian life, *The Truce of God*, contemporary theologian Rowan Williams offers what appears to be a puzzling exemplar of the peacemaker: the monastic. When picturing the kind of persons capable of mediating conflict, we are more apt to turn to the heroic images of the White Hats or of peace negotiators in Syria and Iraq. But Williams turns our attention to the monastics precisely because he thinks that they encapsulate peacemaking in a way that eludes political forms of nonviolence. The monastics, Williams suggests, understand that many of our valiant attempts to make peace are caught in an endless loop of self-justifying jargon, stuck in ruts that only ingrain our conflicts further.[1] In their life of prayer, monks understand that the real struggle is one

1. Williams, *Truce of God*, 55.

of the soul and that any struggle against the powers of death must begin in prayer.[2]

In an age of civil wars, boycotts, and devolving international treaties, Williams's vision can seem like an evasion. It can seem as though mystics are turning inward to the struggle of the soul instead of answering the life-and-death call of the world. From the nineteenth century, mysticism has been characterized as effectively apolitical and unconcerned with social action.[3] But this, mystics contend, is a misunderstanding. For the figures of this chapter, Christian nonviolence depends first and foremost on the experience of the soul with God, not on prudential calculations or on rules of action. In this chapter, we discuss the various structures of mystical encounter and how the encounter with God provides the basis for nonviolence as a practice. To do so, we highlight the approaches to nonviolent mysticism found in the writings of Howard Thurman, Dorothee Sölle, Henri Nouwen, Thomas Merton, and John Dear.

The Mystical Basis of Nonviolence

Nonviolence is often understood as having a primarily political nature, oriented toward either international applications (as with realist nonviolence) or domestic applications (as with nonviolence as political practice). But the best-known proponent of political nonviolence, Martin Luther King Jr., was deeply influenced by the work of a practitioner of mystical nonviolence: Howard Thurman.[4] Thurman, pastor and dean

2. Williams, *Truce of God*, 63–64.

3. The classic articulation of this view is Troeltsch, *Social Teachings of the Christian Churches*, 2:993–1014.

4. The influences on King's nonviolence are manifold and not reducible to one source. On the role of Thurman in King's thought, see Dorrien, "King and His Mentors."

of chapel at Howard University and Boston University, was a one-time Baptist minister deeply involved in struggles against segregation and racism. Inspired by Mohandas Gandhi's work, he was part of a delegation that visited Gandhi in 1935 and brought back Gandhi's vision of nonviolence to America.[5] But unlike some who would later emphasize the tactical nature of Gandhi's vision, such as Gene Sharp,[6] Thurman resonated with the mystical center of Gandhi's thought, viewing it as the center of any cohesive account of nonviolence.

Thurman consistently employed the themes of mysticism and prayer in his writings on social change and conflict. Instead of emphasizing how nonviolence could be an effective tool for de-escalating conflicts or for combatting war, Thurman grounds nonviolence's meaning in mystical contemplation. For Thurman, as for other nonviolent mystics, nonviolence is rooted not in taking political action or calculating effectiveness but in a transformative encounter of the soul with God. It is only in such an encounter with God, as Thurman sees it, that the soul opens up a new way of living in the world.[7]

For nonviolent mystics, the mystical basis for nonviolence addresses the deepest sources of our conflict—our distorted vision of ourselves and of God. Yet this basis is difficult to articulate, for as Dorothee Sölle writes, mysticism is "an experience of God, an experience of being one with God . . . that breaks through the existing limitations of human comprehension, feeling and reflection."[8] In other words, unlike other approaches to nonviolence, mysticism does not immediately generate a

5. For this history, see Dixie and Eisenstadt, *Visions of a Better World*; Azaransky, *This Worldwide Struggle*.

6. See Sharp's *Politics of Nonviolent Action* trilogy.

7. For a full exposition of Thurman on mysticism, see Thurman, "Mysticism and Social Change"; Thurman, *Creative Encounter*.

8. Sölle, *Strength of the Weak*, 86–87.

community of advocates or supporters, in part because the basis of our peace is not one object among others. For the mystics, our union is in the God who is beyond language, beyond being captured as an idol.

Although slipping beyond human comprehension makes the encounter with God difficult to speak of, it is also why mysticism promises peace where politics cannot. For Thurman, in the mystical encounter of prayer one transcends the doctrinal particularities that divide Christians—or that divide one faith's claims about the nature of God from another's—and centers one's attention and being on God, the source of all existence. One also, through such prayer, unites the whole of the one praying before God.[9] This experience before God, for Thurman, reaches the core of the issue of violence: the self-righteous and egoistic self.[10] In the encounter with God, who is love, the self-righteous ego is given no place to hide and is displaced from its throne, with the ego replaced by the desire for the unity and beauty of God. People who see themselves according to one set of descriptions are confronted with their true selves before God and given a new sense of self—one rooted in their common unity with other members of creation.

Thurman writes that our conflicts—both political and interpersonal—are self-perpetuating, as the wounded conform to their wounding, repeating the wounds we receive from others in an endless desire for revenge.[11] The mystical encounter with God, by contrast, replaces our self-righteous need for vindication with a desire for union because the soul has witnessed the love of God. In the mystical encounter of prayer and

9. Thurman, *Creative Encounter*, 197: "It is reasonable to suggest then that such knowledge is essentially more real and it touches and partakes of reality at a deeper point than the knowledge attained by the processes of discursive logic."

10. Thurman, *Deep Is the Hunger*, 133.

11. Thurman, *Deep Is the Hunger*, 88.

meditation, one is joined with God in a way that imprints on the soul unity where there was previously division, the undivided love of God where there was previously self-absorption.[12] This, Thurman writes, gives birth to a new *ethical* unity that is not automatic, that must be struggled for, but that ultimately is the result of being made a "new creature" because of what one has experienced in God.[13]

Thurman's mysticism finds echoes in the work of Henri Nouwen, Catholic priest and author who spent much of his life among poor communities in Peru and later with L'Arche communities among the disabled. Nouwen is perhaps best known for his emphasis on ministers as "wounded healers," but what is less known is that this concept of woundedness in our encounters with God centered his thought on poverty and violence. Speaking at a Vietnam War protest rally in 1972, Nouwen put it this way: "If we want to respond to the incredible violence in our world with a credible nonviolence, we have to be willing to realize that nonviolence is not a technique to conquer peace, but a deep personal attitude which makes it possible to receive peace as a gift. . . . Let us therefore go forth in the peace which the world cannot give, a peace we want to share with each other and with everyone we meet on our way."[14]

For Nouwen, it is indispensable to recall that peace, as Rowan Williams reminds us, is a gift of God, one to be received and not manufactured. As we see in Thurman, our manufactured unities conceal deep wounds, wounds that—unless laid bare—will only perpetuate further conflicts.

For Nouwen and Thurman, the encounter with God alters the soul in a way that changes our ethical posture toward others.

12. Thurman, *Meditations of the Heart*, 25.
13. Thurman, "Mysticism and Social Change," 210.
14. Nouwen, "No to Vietnam," 67–68.

For these writers, nonviolence is the *ethical conclusion* of the encounter with God, but nonviolence is not the *content* of the encounter with God. As Thomas Merton, a Trappist priest steeped in Catholic Social Teaching, frames it, contemplation is the event of the "person [deepening] their own thoughts in silence, [entering] into a deeper understanding and communion with the spirit of [one's] entire people,"[15] but this is not to say that this communion immediately generates ethical positions. The contemplative encounter with God in prayer displaces our ego, reframing our vision of ourselves in light of God and God's creation, but it does not immediately bear itself out in a political program. The value of this approach is that it refuses to move to nonviolence as a practical act, humbly recognizing that what is at stake in nonviolence is not only quieting forms of violence in the world but also addressing the root of violence: the disordered and disquieted soul. As such, there is a distance between the encounter with God and how this encounter bears out in the world.

In contrast to a realist nonviolence rooted in prudential reason and calculation, nonviolent mystics generally express a deep suspicion regarding whether our reasons for engaging in conflict can be trusted or whether our fear, passions, and self-deception are shaping our reasons for conflict. Only through the act of contemplation, of placing ourselves before God, are we laid open to the truth of both ourselves and God—truth that runs counter to violence, revealing our lives with others to be shot through with ego and power. As Williams points out, the mysticism of prayer bears the weakness of not being immediately pressed into service to a political plan, but this is also mysticism's strength: the mystical encounter with God orients us toward creation's unity rather than allowing us to return to caring for only a faction of the world.

15. Merton, *Gandhi on Nonviolence*, 6.

From the Self to the World

The connection between one's prayerful encounter with God and one's actions in the world appears counterintuitive, until viewed in light of the biographies of these practitioners. Thurman writes much of his work on mysticism and violence in the midst of his struggles against segregation. Nouwen begins to explore themes of nonviolence and prayer while on a six-month journey in South America amid poverty and violence. Sölle and Merton write on mysticism and nonviolence amid the struggles of post-war Germany and Vietnam, respectively. For all of them, the mystical experience with God points to the core of both violence and the ability of the Christian to remain present to the suffering of violence. As Merton notes,

> As soon as I say, "God exists," my existence no longer can remain in the center, because the essence of the knowledge of God reveals my own existence as deriving its total being from his. This is the true conversion experience. . . . Then it becomes real for me that I can love myself and my neighbor only because God has loved me first. . . . Once I "know" God, that is, once I experience his love as the love in which all my human experiences are anchored, I can only desire one thing: to be in that love. "Being" anywhere else, then, is shown to be illusory and eventually lethal.[16]

This encounter with God is likewise primary for Thurman, for it alone is the peace that Jesus spoke of, and it alone heals the deep wounding of egoism and violence.[17] But the world in which the mystic lives remains one of violence and wounding. Here Thurman's mysticism seeks to apply its vision: if the love

16. Merton, *Gandhi on Nonviolence*, 48.
17. Thurman, *Growing Edge*, 1–28.

of God is central for us, then that which moves us away from this encounter with God must be opposed. Society must be affected, not to usher in a utopia but to remove that which is blocking all people from encountering God, as patterned for the Christian by Jesus.[18]

Nonviolence for Thurman, then, is first the necessary outworking and witness of one's encounter with God. In light of the unity and love of God, egoism (the source of conflict) is displaced by God's love, a love that must be mirrored and enacted interpersonally and socially. But, second, nonviolence also has a preparatory work, for it is only through nonviolent means that one can properly remove those things that block all people from a true encounter with God. Segregation, for example, would be undone not by returning violence with violence but by suffering, self-sacrifice, and speaking truthfully. Racial conflict would be undone not by further bloodshed but by placing the good of one's enemy over one's own survival.[19] In other words, the way that mirrors God (nonviolence) must cohere to what one receives from God (love).

But for Nouwen the connection made with God through the mystical encounter—though transformative of the mystic—produces "a spirituality that allows us to live in the world without belonging to it, a spirituality that allows us to taste the joy and peace of the divine life even when we are surrounded by the powers and principalities of evil, death, and destruction."[20] As Nouwen ministered in a context closely associated with liberation theology, he saw how the move toward societal transformation—as intrinsically necessitated by the mystical life—threatened to instrumentalize the encounter with God. Thus while Thurman emphasized removing the blocks that opposed

---

18. Thurman, "Significance of Jesus."
19. Thurman, *Jesus and the Disinherited*, 69–73.
20. Nouwen, *¡Gracias!*, 12.

the mystical encounter for all persons, whether Christian or not, Nouwen worked to nourish that life within others from his pastoral vocation, within a liturgical framework, and to let the response to violence be rooted in personal transformation, not social modification.[21]

The mystical encounter with God led its proponents into a wide variety of activities. Whereas Thurman drew out the implications of the mystical life for the spiritual roots of segregation and war, Nouwen turned his attention to the dynamics of prayer in a more liturgical setting, writing about how the mystical life counteracted ministers' abuses of power.[22] For Nouwen, the mystical encounter with God found its outworking in consistent identification with the suffering and powerless, as those among whom God was most directly at work. For Thurman, the mystical encounter must be coupled with the removal of social structures (segregation and war, most immediately) that stifle this central mystical encounter with God among both the oppressor and the oppressed, through their proliferation of practices of division and hatred.[23]

While Nouwen, Thurman, and Merton emphasize the relation between the contemplative self and their life in the world, what remains obscured in their work is how, for men and women, the social engagements coming out of the mystical encounter with God might differ. Sölle, as a feminist mystic,

21. In *¡Gracias!*, Nouwen recounts his own conversations with liberationist Jon Sobrino while working in El Salvador and the tension that Nouwen felt between his own mystical approach and that of Sobrino (64–66). See also Nouwen, "Celebrating Life," 42: "I therefore want to say here as clearly as I can that the first and foremost task of the peacemaker is not to fight death but to call forth, affirm, and nurture the signs of life wherever they become manifest." This is not to say that Nouwen rejects the active practice of nonviolence; he sees it as essential to building communities, as in Nouwen, *Peacework*. But for Nouwen, social transformation remains secondary to the transformation of the self.

22. Nouwen, *Path of Power*.

23. Compare Nouwen, *Selfless Way of Christ*, with Thurman, *Luminous Darkness*.

directs attention to the specifically gendered ways a violent society operates. If Christians seek to oppose the powers and principalities of the world, Sölle observes, they cannot do so without recognizing the ways society disproportionately exercises violence toward women, often by using a theology that justifies their oppression.[24] For Sölle, we open ourselves to God in prayer, and in doing so, we both locate our identity within the true source of the self (God) and find that the true identification of God as beyond gender is necessary for the subjugation of women to cease.[25]

Connecting Mysticism and Nonviolence

Nonviolent mystics broadly refuse to mobilize mystical prayer for some other purpose, letting nonviolence instead be the consequence of the encounter with God. But for each nonviolent mystic we have considered, the connection between the encounter with a God who quiets the conflict within the soul and bearing this out in the world is undeniable. For Nouwen, the mystical encounter with God in Christ leads most directly to solidarity with the suffering—those who have been wounded by poverty, war, or some other kind of psychic wounding. To extend the healing of Christ to the world, one must tarry with those who have been wounded, offering Christ's love in the manner *of* Christ.[26] Nonviolence is thus an act that is embodied as a result of the mystical encounter:

24. See Sölle, *Strength of the Weak*, 79–117, for her explication of this theme.

25. Sölle advocates the use of male and female names for God, not as a way of "balancing things out" but as logically following from the mystical recognition of God as beyond gender. See Sölle, *Strength of the Weak*, 114–17.

26. Though we discuss liberation theology in chapter 7, the division between mysticism and liberation thinkers is not solid, and the doxological commitments most pronounced here are amply present throughout liberationist writings. See Prevot, *Thinking Prayer*, 165–325, for discussions of James Cone, Leonardo Boff, Gustavo Gutiérrez, and others.

the Christian proceeds into the world seeking to live in a manner consistent with the encounter one has had with God. Likewise, in Merton's work we find consistent connection between the mystical life and a world at war, with Christians bearing witness to the transfiguring love of God in their engagements with non-Christians or those from countries other than their own.[27]

One concern with this approach is that mysticism does too much work by claiming that whatever peace is encountered with God mandates a particular form of nonviolent social practice. Merton takes up this concern. He argues that it is not the case that nonviolence is self-evidently consistent with God's internal character or that it is in the act of nonviolence that one meets God. Rather, for Merton the contemplative act exposes just war thinking as inherently problematic, as the just war approach makes too much out of "natural law" and the demands of realism and makes too little out of the substance of the peaceable contemplative life embodied in Jesus's wisdom.[28] The approach toward violence that Jesus commends is not centered on stopping all possible forms of violence and turns not on "the conversion of the wicked to the ideas of the good" but is rather "for the healing and reconciliation of man with himself, man the person and man the human family." Merton emphasizes that it is only by "faith in Christ the Redeemer and obedience to his demand to love and manifest himself in us in a certain manner of acting in the world and in relation to other" humans that such an act of nonviolence is possible. The Holy Spirit, acting "in us, not for our own

27. Merton, "Christian as Peacemaker," 27–34.

28. For Merton's criticisms of the just war paradigm, see his essay "Christian Action in World Crisis." See also Sölle, *Arms Race Kills Even without War*, 4–5, in which she claims that preparation for war both justifies present suffering and deprives future generations of material goods they would need to thrive.

good alone but for God and his kingdom," provides the sole basis for nonviolence.[29]

The connection of nonviolence to mystical prayer is one of cause and undeniable effect, transformation of the heart coupled with an undeniable conclusion for one's social practice. But for some, such as prolific Jesuit author John Dear, nonviolence is the sacrament by which the mystical encounter itself occurs. It is not only the *outworking* of the mystical encounter but also the *context* of the mystical encounter. Reflecting on nonviolent civil disobedience, Dear writes, "If we act with predisposed, open, loving hearts, then we will experience the grace of God's spirit working through us. We may not fully understand what is happening, but we will sense that God is present. . . . Though we will probably not know the 'effect' of our symbolic activity, this felt presence of God's love in us will sustain us to trust in God with real hope and to continue along the Way of the Gospels."[30]

Here, true to the mystical encounter, practitioners engage in an activity that they do not truly understand, and in doing so, they are grasped by the God who transforms that activity. For Dear, this mode of action takes a variety of forms—protests, ecological care, civil disobedience, prison reform—but in each of these forms, he sees people engaging with God through the practice of nonviolence.[31] In contrast to Nouwen, for whom nonviolence is the *consequence* of the mystical encounter, for Dear the nonviolent act is inextricable from meeting God. The two come into focus together.[32]

29. Merton, "Blessed Are the Meek," 249, 250.
30. Dear, *Sacrament of Civil Disobedience*, 154–55.
31. Dear, *They Will Inherit the Earth*; Dear, *Peace behind Bars*.
32. For Dear, prayer prepares one to be able to discern the mode of nonviolence and prepares the heart for the encounter itself. But it is the act itself—and specifically, what is encountered in the act—that encourages the need for preparation in

For Dear, the ethics of nonviolence and the God who is encountered are inseparable, for it is through nonviolence that the
encounter with God happens. God is revealed to us in Jesus as
the nonviolent God, Dear argues, a truth that we can now see
in the dynamics of the trinitarian life.[33] Early Christians understood God as "an interrelating, communal God who is one and
who is three [who] led them to form communities of nonviolent
resistance to evil and cooperation with that Spirit."[34] Accordingly, when one encounters God in prayer, the God encountered
is dispossessive and noncoercive. Merton, in contrast, found
these kinds of equations problematic; for him nonviolence must
always be born out of the humble encounter with God, and
the temptation toward nonviolence as befitting a divine pattern runs the risk of grasping nonviolence while leaving the
encounter with God behind.[35]

Merton's criticisms notwithstanding, embracing nonviolence as intrinsic to the mystical encounter with God need not
be a utopic vision. Just because one encounters the beauty of
God in prayer does not mean that the world will reflect that
beauty. A world of violence is one that is caught up in suffering, and those who commit themselves to nonviolence must
embrace that suffering. As Sölle puts it, "The bitter Christ is
experienced in a discipleship of suffering. Suffering, not just
believing, is the way to God." By saying this, Sölle is not justifying the suffering of the world, embracing an invisible goodness
and ignoring the injustices of the world. Rather, she is pointing

---

prayer. See Dear, *Sacrament*, 165–90; Dear, *They Will Inherit the Earth*, 104–6; Dear,
Disarming the Heart, 56–63.

33. Dear, *God of Peace*, 33–51. Faced with the Old Testament passages that offer a
more violent view of God's activity in the world, Dear cites Walter Wink, who writes,
"This violence is in part the residue of false ideas about God carried over from the
general human past" (34).

34. Dear, *God of Peace*, 46.

35. Merton, *Faith and Violence*, 16.

us to the ways in which prayer opens us to the strength that enables people not simply to bear up under suffering but also to embrace it as a source of genuine strength.[36]

There is a kind of masochism that both society and certain forms of Christianity encourage, Sölle observes, in which suffering turns the sufferer into a passive, impotent subject. But those who suffer, she says, are engaging in a companionship with Christ that those who do not suffer cannot understand. For Sölle, the mystical way points not in the direction of avoiding or justifying suffering but "in the opposite direction: the soul is open to suffering, abandons itself to suffering, holds back nothing." It is here that the soul, like Job, receives suffering as an unjust visitor and speaks to God about this injustice, joining with the Jesus who suffers. To join in the nonviolence of Jesus, then, is to join in the suffering of God on behalf of the world and to follow Christ in his claim that he and the Father are one. This unity, for nonviolent mystics, suggests that embracing suffering is an essential part of what it means for God to redeem the world.[37]

Conclusion

Among the nonviolent mystics discussed in this chapter, there emerges a broad consensus but also disagreement. They broadly agree that, in the words of Merton, war is rooted in "the appetites and disorder in your own soul" and that any response to war must retrace its steps beyond the political frameworks that enable conflict to happen.[38] Those who turn to contemplation, prayer, and meditation find in the encounter with

---

36. Sölle, *Suffering*, 129–30, 149.
37. Sölle, *Suffering*, 24, 101, 118, 134. On this theme, see also Weil, *Gravity and Grace*, 137–45.
38. Merton, "Root of War Is Fear."

God a dethroning of the self and an invitation to dwell in the presence of the peaceable God. But disagreement emerges precisely with how to name the content of the mystical encounter. For Nouwen mysticism means an encounter with the person of Christ. Encountering the risen Christ in prayer drives one deeper into imitation of Christ's way in the world. In contrast, for Thurman the mystical encounter is an encounter with the mystery of God beyond Christ, and limiting the vision of God to an exclusively Christian one is part of what contributes to division and conflict in the world.

Likewise, the implications of the mystical encounter for nonviolence are varied. For some, the implications are deeply interpersonal, as seen in the writings of Nouwen. But for others, as with Thurman and Sölle, the implications are undeniably political, for the encounter with God calls for nothing less than a transformation of the heart of the modern world, removing the socially constructed roadblocks to God (Thurman) and razing the idols that run counter to the mystical heart of God (Sölle). For Merton and Thurman, the implications involve reconciliation of Christians with non-Christians, as Christians become willing to learn from non-Christians as bearers of what has been glimpsed in the life of prayer.[39]

39. Merton, *Signs of Peace*.

Apocalyptic Nonviolence

EXPOSING THE POWER OF DEATH

When Christian nonviolence is imagined, often images of a civil street protest come to mind. For many—particularly those of the civil rights movement and Vietnam War eras—this was the predominant image. But as the Vietnam War dragged on, those engaging in traditional routes of nonviolent activism against the war—marches, protests, petitions—began to grow weary. It was not that nonviolence had been ineffective in those years, as the civil rights movement attests. Rather, there was a growing sense that the theological dimensions of nonviolence were being blunted. During this period, a number of people, such as Vincent Harding and James Cone, began to argue for a more radical approach to the struggle for civil rights. They remained critical interlocutors for proponents of nonviolence by helping to clarify whether nonviolent action was intrinsic to the revolution needed to overturn the civic and religious powers more comfortable with the frequently moderate approach of earlier civil rights leaders.[1]

The problem was not that nonviolence itself is unworkable; instead, the concern was that, by framing nonviolence in terms of what government entities could hear, the radicalism of nonviolence was being sidelined. James F. Childress, in his landmark *Civil Disobedience and Political Obligation*, frames legitimate forms of nonviolence as those that are "public, nonviolent, submissive violations of law," a definition that a priori rules out actions that do not "communicate" to government and that use force or seek to coerce their opponent.[2] But as critics of nonviolent opposition have pointed out, this turns nonviolence into an acquiescent political voice, dependent on a benevolent government to set the terms by which it will be addressed.[3] Beyond this, it assumes that the legal paradigm enabling war can adequately set the terms for discussing violence.

On May 17, 1968, nine Catholic activists opened a different avenue for nonviolence. Going to the Selective Service office in Catonsville, Maryland, these activists took several hundred draft records and set them ablaze in the parking lot, using homemade napalm. This initial action would be followed by many others across the country and began to be known as "plowshares" actions, for their actions were akin to the biblical motif of beating swords (instruments of war) into plowshares (farming tools).[4] In destroying implements

---

1. See in particular Cone's comments in *God of the Oppressed*, 179–206; and Harding's interview in Shenk, *Movement Makes Us Human*, 55–66.

2. Childress, *Civil Disobedience and Political Obligation*, 11.

3. Gelderloos, *How Nonviolence Protects the State*.

4. For a history of the Plowshares movement, see Nepstad, *Religion and War Resistance in the Plowshares Movement*.

of war—whether in the form of draft cards, armaments, or nuclear weapons—this approach began to confront the means of war more actively. Instead of lobbying or marching, this approach—what we here call *apocalyptic nonviolence*—emphasizes the conflict between Christ's way of life and the world's way of Death.[5]

In subsequent years, figures like William Stringfellow, Daniel Berrigan, and René Girard articulated a new vision for nonviolence that is less directly concerned with being included within a robust democratic process and more committed to how nonviolence exposes the rot within the system it opposes. Apocalyptic nonviolence takes as its starting point not only that the cross and resurrection of Jesus unveil the powers and principalities of the world for what they are but also that Jesus's death and resurrection call for Christians to actively oppose the machinations of Death in the world.

Many familiar conversations surrounding nonviolence—such as whether nonviolence is tactically feasible or whether it makes us more virtuous—are secondary for apocalyptic nonviolence. Instead, what is primary to apocalyptic nonviolence is the guiding conviction that nonviolence continues the work of God in Christ, which exposes Death for what it is. As such, apocalyptic nonviolence is more confrontational in nature, in keeping with what is at stake: the contest between the resurrection life of Jesus and the power of Death.

5. Following a practice common among apocalyptic theologians, we capitalize the word *Death* when referring to it not merely as cessation of life but as an active power in the world that stands in opposition to God. As with the other movements we discuss, apocalyptic theology is a living and dynamic movement that we cannot do full justice to in this chapter. By focusing on those figures who best exemplify this form of Christian nonviolence, we elide other major figures in the movement, such as German theologian and New Testament scholar Ernst Käsemann. See, for example, Käsemann, *Church Conflicts*. For an introduction to apocalyptic theology, see Ziegler, *Militant Grace*.

The Struggle (Not) against Flesh and Blood

The central theological commitment of apocalyptic nonviolence is not that Christ's life provides a model for nonviolence, as with nonviolence of Christian discipleship, but rather that Christ's death and resurrection expose the power of Death itself. The death and resurrection of Christ do not merely inspire us to act but are carried forward, by the power of the Spirit, in the bodies and actions of Christians today. As such, the contest between Death and Christ, though definitively ended in Jesus's work, continues through the actions of Christians, those who join the revolution against the powers and principalities.

If we focus on the question of what kind of war is justified, William Stringfellow argues, we miss the basic issue: war itself is one of the many principalities by which Death continues to rule human life.[6] According to Stringfellow, the various idols throughout society that lead us away from God are motivated by one single power: Death. There is no safe place from Death, either in justified war or (importantly) in ideological pacifism, which seeks to wash its hands of the world.[7] The battle we fight against Death in our private lives—whether on the front of sexual morality, bodily decay, cultural idolatry, or war—is all part of the same fight.[8]

Walter Wink's work offers a detailed scriptural backdrop to this theme, narrating the biblical language of "powers and principalities" not as invisible angelic realities but as structural realities animated by spiritual principles. While a business

6. Stringfellow, *Free in Obedience*, 62: "The fall is not just the estate in which men reject God and exalt themselves. . . . The fall is also the awareness of men of their estrangement from God, themselves, each other, and all things, and their pathetic search for God or some substitute for God . . . in the principalities and in the rest of creation."

7. Stringfellow, *Ethic for Christians and Other Aliens in a Strange World*, 82–84, 92.

8. See Stringfellow, *Imposters of God*, for his expanded argument on this point.

corporation, for example, is made up of procedures, policies, and personnel, its immaterial spirit and ethos is what gives it direction, purpose, and shape, far beyond any individual action its employees take. The same, Wink writes, is true of nations and entities of any corporate nature. The powers, which are the "inner aspect of material reality," can only be engaged in their material form, but they are not reducible to their material form.[9]

In this way, in struggling against the powers of Death— manifested in armies, draft apparatuses, or any of the "emissaries" of Death, as Stringfellow puts it—we are engaging not simply material structures but also the demonic spirit animating their actions. They are termed *demonic* not because they worship devils or have satanic rituals but because their actions—in proliferating Death—join in the work of Death willingly. But opposing the powers of Death is not as simple as *only* being opposed to one isolated instance, such as marching against a war or refusing to sign up for the draft. One must also be on guard for the other faces of idolatry that likewise promise to save us from Death, such as proper governmental policies, ideological pacifism, and overly optimistic social movements. For Stringfellow in particular, the powers move people toward Death in manifold ways, such that opposing them requires great discernment. Freedom, then, comes from a refusal to trust in any deliverance from Death other than God in Christ, as one engaged in concrete struggle against the powers.[10]

In a sharp divergence from political pacifism, which tends to emphasize the cultivation of a democratic polity and social policy as a deterrent to war, Stringfellow maintains a much

9. Wink, *Naming the Powers*, 105.
10. Stringfellow, *Keeper of the Word*, 69.

more nefarious vision of the role of government. Writing in the wake of the arrest of the Berrigan brothers—who had been among the "Catonsville Nine" who burned Vietnam War draft cards in an act of protest—Stringfellow writes that "the State has only one power it can use against human beings: death. The state can persecute you, prosecute you, imprison you, exile you, execute you. All of these mean the same thing."[11] Put differently, the state, which promises to deliver us from the violence of war, does so only to dominate human life and, thus, to drive it toward Death a different way.

Destroying the Tools of Violence

One of the distinctive features of apocalyptic nonviolence is its view of what counts as violence. In its most common forms, nonviolence pertains to the refusal to kill another human or to general opposition to war.[12] Because nonviolence seeks, broadly, to foster peace within creation, it has also been extended to refusal to destroy property and physical belongings. Apocalyptic nonviolence, however, troubles this assumption by asking not only what counts as violence but also whether some forms of destruction are *intrinsic* to being nonviolent. If nonviolence is fundamentally about refraining from all forms of harm and destruction, then actions such as what took place in Catonsville, Maryland, in May 1968 are inconsistent with nonviolence. But if nonviolence is about bearing witness in dramatic form to God's overturning of a violent order, then destruction of the *means* of violence—burning draft cards, destroying weapons,

11. Stringfellow, *Second Birthday*, 133.
12. This focus on human life has been challenged by some who argue that excluding nonhuman life from a vision of nonviolence is insufficient. See Camosy, *For the Love of Animals*; Nussburger, "Vegetarianism"; York and Alexis-Baker, *Faith Embracing All Creatures*.

boycotting military manufacturers, and so on—is part of affirming nonviolence.

Since the struggle against Death is one that must be carried on bodily, it follows for Stringfellow that the question *Is violence right?* is the wrong question to ask. Sometimes this question is put to nonviolence as a way of suggesting that being opposed to war is the same thing as marching with Martin Luther King Jr. on the road to Selma. Stringfellow—and his friends in the Catonsville Nine—distinguished between destruction done to property and violence done to persons. Stringfellow, for example, pointed to more explicit forms of protest, such as the Watts riots against police brutality and self-immolations of Vietnam War protesters. Stringfellow did not consider these kinds of acts to be violent since violence always points to Death and seeks to subjugate life; to burn down a building or set oneself on fire is rather a prophetic act designed to illustrate the gravity of what is at stake in the struggle against Death.[13]

Daniel Berrigan, for example, was not in favor of the actions of the Weathermen, an underground radical group in the 1970s who engaged in a series of bombings and plots to break prisoners out of jail. Berrigan saw their actions as simply the inverse of war, opposing violence with violence.[14] In contrast, destroying draft cards—opposing the material means that were supporting war—is much in line with what Walter Wink proposes: that opposition to Death happens as we oppose the material forms of Death. Burning draft cards, writes Berrigan, is part of "trying to live in a way that points to the future and indicates the direction I believe we must all take."[15]

13. Stringfellow, "Ethics of Violence."
14. Berrigan, *Geography of Faith*, 61–62.
15. Berrigan, *Geography of Faith*, 77.

For Berrigan, to be Christian is to embody the judgment of God against the world's violence and to point—by active opposition to violence and the tools of violence—to the way of God in the world.

The Plowshares movement, for example, emphasized symbolic actions in its protests, which would dramatize the conflict between the way of God and the way of Death. Taking its name from the prophet Isaiah's vision of swords being beaten into farming tools (Isa. 2:4), the group was started by Philip Berrigan (Daniel's brother and fellow Catholic priest) and was involved in numerous actions similar to those of the Catonsville Nine. The Plowshares members utilized tactics such as burglarizing an FBI office, hammering on warplanes and nuclear warheads, burning draft cards, and refusing to pay taxes in support of the Vietnam War. But none of these actions were designed first and foremost to influence lawmakers, though opposing unjust laws drew attention to their injustice. Indeed, the penalties levied against Plowshares members were often severe relative to the damage done. Rather, these dramatic actions were meant to enact the ways of God over against Death by quite literally beating a weapon into some other implement and by destroying those things that were assaulting human life.

As Jacques Ellul points out, the justification for violence within society—whether mimetic or structural—rests on the assumption that violence is the first word about creation, its ontological fabric. Once conflict assumes a primary place in our imagination, then all other justifications of violence—its material outworkings and the ways we try to manage it technologically—become perfectly logical and make any appeal to nonviolence inconceivable. Speaking of a God who loves all creation undoes this appeal to violence at the core. The Spirit,

Ellul writes, frees us from the "necessity" of violence by shattering the fatalities and necessities we assume are simply part of what it means to live in the world.[16]

Revealing the Power of Death

As we will see in chapter 6, political nonviolence turns in part on the tactical use of nonviolence, not only because it "works" in its context but also because confronting violence with nonviolence pricks the conscience of the violent oppressor.[17] Apocalyptic nonviolence, by contrast, is premised not on convincing the public or pricking the conscience of the violent but on revealing violence for what it is. In emphasizing public and dramatic forms of destroying the implements of Death, apocalyptic nonviolence is reminiscent more of the prophet Jeremiah, who embodied the destruction about to befall Jerusalem, than of Micah or Amos, who uttered straightforward judgments.

Those who practice apocalyptic nonviolence are thus less interested in changing laws than in bearing witness to two contrasting visions: God's intentions for the world and the self-justifying ways of violence in the world. Thus, in a series of books, theorist René Girard describes how Jesus's death pronounced a judgment on Death and exposed Death for what it is. Human society functions through a kind of mimesis, or imitative practice gone wrong, Girard argues. Not only do we imitate good things; we also imitate with a desire to be better than the one we are imitating. This jealous kind of imitation

16. Ellul, *Violence*, 61, 75, 127–29.
17. Other activists were skeptical of this. As Stokely Carmichael states, "Dr. King's policy was, if you are nonviolent, if you suffer, your opponent will see your suffering and will be moved to change his heart. That's very good. He only made one fallacious assumption. In order for nonviolence to work, your opponent must have a conscience. The United States has none." Olsson, *Black Power Mixtape*.

leads to rivalries, competitions, and, ultimately, communities at war with themselves.[18]

However, rather than resolve the real problems of competition, Girard argues, we hide the violence and foist it on an innocent victim: a scapegoat. This scapegoat becomes the stand-in for all our troubles. If we just get rid of this person or these people, we reason, we can restore peace. Jesus becomes this kind of scapegoat, the one on whom all the troubles of Israel are blamed. But because Jesus was innocent, his death exposes this system of competition, mimesis, and Death for what it is. By condemning to death an innocent victim, the systems that conspired to crucify Jesus are exposed as corrupted.[19] Jesus's death thereby not only embodies a judgment on the unjust, death-dealing ways of the world but also embodies a revelation of how God opposes these things: an embodied refusal of the logic of Death operative in society. The exposure and destruction of the ways of Death and the nonviolence of Jesus go hand in hand, in that the bodily witness of Jesus refutes Death's logic.

The Death that Jesus exposes permeates the world not only in physical decay and justified forms of violence but also in the forms of reasoning that build violence into our daily habits and routines: incarceration, militarism, economic disparity, and structuralized injustices.[20] To oppose these things is not to simply negate them but also, as Daniel Berrigan puts it, to "indicate the direction" of the new life. William Desmond argues that to act in this way is to be consecrated by primal peace itself, the

18. Girard, "Mimesis and Violence."

19. Girard, *Things Hidden since the Foundation of the World*, 180–215.

20. Sullivan and Boehrer, "Practice of Nonviolence in the Contemporary World." In this interview with Berrigan, the loci he names are reminiscent of Martin Luther King Jr.'s speech "Beyond Vietnam," which was penned in large part by Vincent Harding. See Shenk, *Movement Makes Us Human*, xv, xviii.

true logic of the world, that we might be faithful witnesses to the reality of creation that violence seeks to undermine.[21]

This violence is most evident in the physical destruction of other human life, but as Ellul helps us see, modern violence is more frequently carried out by "slow" violences, bureaucratic and internalized forms of dehumanization.[22] Secularized societies are prone to historicization and order, Ellul argues, to perpetuate their ideology and to perfect their visions over time. As such, even secular revolutions—while offering something new on the surface—are simply different ways of increasingly extending the domination of an institution over human life.[23] The truly different kind of revolution, he says, is an apocalyptic one, which refuses the tendency to treat human life like a perfectible product and which keeps human aspirations perpetually open to God's new work and new direction.[24]

To be sure, the Christian Scriptures—both Old and New Testaments—are concerned with the ways human life is undermined by sin. The prophets are quick to name all kinds of things—from militarism to poverty to injustice—as idolatrous aspects of our world that must be overturned. Apocalyptic nonviolence thus reads Jesus as exposing Death for what it is and opposing the violence of the world with his own embodied way of peace. But even if Jesus is the revelation of God to creation, in a way that opposes violence, we are still left with many places in Scripture that commend violence not simply as something the people of God do but also as something that God does on occasion.

For apocalyptic nonviolence, which assumes that the crucifixion exposes violence in the world, one possibility for

21. Desmond, "Consecrating Peace," 112–13.
22. Ellul, *New Demons*, 140–41.
23. Ellul, *New Demons*, 85–86.
24. Ellul, *Presence of the Kingdom*, 30–32.

approaching violent biblical texts, as James Allison argues, is to see Jesus's subversion of his audience's expectations as introducing an eschatological element that was not seen before Christ. In other words, the actions of Jesus open up our understanding of the nature of the biblical texts on violence in ways that would not have been possible before.[25] This approach is similar to that of some patristic exegetes, who considered texts such as the conquest of Canaan to have been spiritual allegories all along.[26] At times, Daniel Berrigan reads texts like 1 Kings as condemnations of military idolatry, but at other times, he raises the possibility that certain Old Testament texts (such as Deut. 28) are simply Israelite propaganda that must be deconstructed.[27] Elsewhere, in discussing Exodus's use of divine violence, Berrigan suggests that part of the prophetic task within Scripture is to subvert these kinds of troubling texts and that Jesus ultimately completes this prophetic subversion.[28]

Thus, in prioritizing the revelatory action of Jesus, the apocalyptic approach to nonviolence has developed various ways to make sense of biblical passages in which God commends violence. Some follow allegorical interpreters such as Origen. Some opt for reading these texts as ancient propaganda, which is undone by the prophets. Some, more provocatively, make the case that God simply changes and undoes past ways, as Berrigan suggests. Thomas Andrew Bennett proposes that, rather than assuming that God changes, we can see in Christ's death a work that is contiguous with what God has always done with

25. Allison, *Raising Abel*.
26. See Origen, *Homilies of Joshua* 14.1: "Unless those physical wars bore the figure of spiritual wars, I do not think the books of Jewish history would ever have been handed down by the apostles to the disciple of Christ, who came to teach peace, so that they could be read in the churches."
27. Berrigan, *No Gods but One*, 148.
28. Berrigan, *Exodus*, 75–96.

respect to violence: transforming something that moves people away from God into something that moves them toward God.[29]

In addition to avoiding some of the Marcionite tendencies in Berrigan, Bennett's proposal also helps us make sense of why burning draft cards can be an act of nonviolence. As Bennett argues, if God repurposes violence in order to transform it in such a way that it brings life, we can see God's actions throughout the Old Testament as repurposing the violence of creation toward the redemptive work of God. In this way, burning draft cards and destroying nuclear weapons are acts of nonviolence that enable us to move toward Christ, while any act of taking human life will always move us away from Christ. Repurposing swords into plowshares is an act of coercing something into a different shape, but it is done so that the violence the object was intended for might bear witness to the peace of God.[30]

Conclusion

For those who practice apocalyptic nonviolence, violence is highly structuralized and disseminated through the stories we tell, how we think of the necessity of certain actions, and how we imagine history is unfolding. As Ellul describes, because we think of our world as having matured beyond God, we engage in a kind of management of it through increasingly refined forms of power, violence, and control. For Ellul, the technological society is the most attractive face of this form of control, but behind it lies a vicious vision of the world: a world that must be managed and controlled in order to confront the violence of the world with yet more violence.[31]

29. Bennett, *Labor of God*, 44–45.
30. For a dramatic contemporary example of repurposing weapons, see Claiborne and Martin, *Beating Guns.*
31. Ellul, *Violence*, 40–47.

The way out of a world of violence—whether in its manage-
rial and bureaucratic forms or in its spontaneous and visceral
forms—is to see all of our lives as always open before God. As
Ellul writes, "A Christian cannot have any other vision of the
world in which he lives than an apocalyptic one; and knowing
very well that historically it is not necessarily the end of the
world, he must act at every moment as if this moment were
the last."[32]

For all the proponents of apocalyptic nonviolence we have
surveyed in this chapter, what nonviolence must do is more than
simply protest or dramatize the conflict between Death and
Christ; it must carve out a new way to be human in the world
that does not presume that violence is the way of creation. To
simply condemn violence is one thing; to create a new space
for being human is another.

One of the difficulties with creating a nonviolent polity is the
notion of boundaries. As Grace Jantzen suggests, boundaries
involve the creation of a body that is exclusive to all others who
do not fall within its boundaries; citizenship, as a matter of belonging, inevitably repeats the violence it is designed to avoid.[33]
Christ, argues Jantzen, breaks the mimetic pattern that simply
moves violence downstream and offers a new way of thinking
about our social relations that is not competitive. Jantzen observes that some say that Christ offers a new narrative—that
the life of Jesus offers people a new script to follow that does
not require the deaths of others—but, for Jantzen, this too can
be exclusionary, which in turn leads to competitiveness and
the same dynamics that fuel Girard's mimesis and violence.
Similarly, apocalyptic theologian Ry Siggelkow argues that
Stanley Hauerwas's ecclesiological pacifism becomes "centrally

---

32. Ellul, *Presence of the Kingdom*, 32.
33. Jantzen, *Violence to Eternity*, 19.

preoccupied with preserving and maintaining—policing—the borders of its community." But, writes Siggelkow, "if the peace to which Christian pacifists witness is reducible to the perdurance of a specific cultural form, then the church's mission to the world becomes a species of ecclesial propaganda. In such a framework, the peace to which the church is committed cannot help but function self-reflexively, in that its witness of peace becomes nothing other than a witness to its own life in which peace is an essential quality. Such an account not only misrepresents the 'peace' to which the church witnesses, theologically; it misrepresents the violence that the world names, biblically."[34]

A truly new kind of ecclesial politic, Jantzen and Siggelkow suggest, is one that is always new and that listens to the margins of its vision to ensure that its vision does not become simply another kind of bureaucracy.[35] The temptation identified here—that a politics that offers something new simply repeats the divisions of the old world in a different way—is one that Ellul and Stringfellow also identify. In calling for a new kind of politics, Stringfellow says that our common life—if it were to escape Death—must always listen for God's new voice in our midst.[36] The Berrigan brothers, likewise, promoted new democratic movements that keep open space for God to disrupt our patterns. But it was Paul Lehmann who articulated what a truly new politics of this manner might entail on the ground.

In Lehmann's *The Transfiguration of Politics*, he argues for a form of politics that already has the eschatological vindication of God in view. If God's throne is surrounded by the martyrs who have died rather than take the life of another, as Ellul argues in his commentary on Revelation, then any politic that

34. Siggelkow, "Toward an Apocalyptic Peace Church," 276.
35. Jantzen, *Violence to Eternity*, 55; Siggelkow, "Toward an Apocalyptic Peace Church," 296.
36. See Werntz, "Ubiquity of Christ and the Sites of Redemption," 260–74.

seeks to bear witness to Christ must have this vision in view and be conformed to its image.[37] Lehmann writes, "Eschatology sets beginnings under a promise that has ruptured the chain of cause and effect and broken open a future that has liberated freedom from the paralysis of the past."[38] Girard and Ellul both identify this "chain of cause and effect" as the imaginative vice that keeps us from seeing any politic other than one undergirded by violence. This is also why the Berrigans thought it so important to expose Death for what it is.

A new kind of revolution, Lehmann argues, is what is needed to begin exposing Death. But, as Ellul argues, revolution must not simply replace one kind of determinism with another. Rather, a new kind of revolution—one originating in love— would be a kind of "permanent revolution," a revolution that would not inflict violence in the struggle to overturn the mechanisms of Death. Christians are not to shy away from confrontation. Rather than receiving confrontations "as a sign of the necessity of violence," they are to receive them as a sign "of the dehumanizing dynamics of the society in which violence has become endemic."[39] In other words, when the revolution Lehmann describes arrives, it will be greeted with violence as a sign that the old order is in its last days. Apocalyptic nonviolence, in first signifying what the existing order is built on, creates space for a new kind of world that refuses the deterministic logic of the existing order, which sees no way to live other than the way of Death. As we will see in the next chapter, this is a different kind of outcome than a realist nonviolence that hopes to transform the existing arrangements in a more just direction.

37. Ellul, *Apocalypse*.
38. Lehmann, *Transfiguration of Politics*, 13.
39. Lehmann, *Transfiguration of Politics*, 266.

Realist Nonviolence

CREATING JUST PEACE IN A FALLEN WORLD

In the late nineteenth and early twentieth centuries, as Christians associated with the social gospel movement began applying Christian principles to society writ large, an international movement to abolish war coalesced. As David Cortright describes, "The expanding networks of peace advocacy began to reach significant scale by the turn of the twentieth century," and "the international peace movement reached the apogee of its public influence and support in the years immediately preceding World War I." Cortright calls this period "a golden age for peace."[1]

This golden age for peace came to a crashing halt with the onset of the Great War. Many within the social gospel movement became convinced that peace could only be established by fighting one last "war to end all wars," and they thereby abandoned their earlier pacifist positions in support of the war effort. In the aftermath of this devastating world war,

1. Cortright, *Peace*, 25, 43.

theologian Reinhold Niebuhr emerged as a critic of the peace movement of which he had earlier been a part. He argued that the pacifism of the social gospel movement was predicated on naive optimism about the possibilities of human societies—an optimism thoroughly discredited by the war. According to his Christian realism, Christ provides the absolute moral ideal, but humans—especially human societies—are incapable of achieving this ideal as a result of sin. When taking account of human sinfulness, moral absolutes become elusive and moral compromises become necessary. For Niebuhr, such moral compromises include the willingness to use violent force to combat greater evils of tyranny or anarchy.[2]

Christian realism has long been associated with Niebuhr's thought—and with good cause, as Niebuhr was its most prominent proponent. But Christian realism has also always been broader than Niebuhr and his disciples. Rather than equating Christian realism with a particular ethical position, especially on the question of violence, we view it as a mode of ethical deliberation that seeks the best course of action amid the tension between the eschatological ideal of the kingdom of God and the realities of fallen societies. As Robin Lovin writes, Christian realism is a "way of thinking" that holds that "social achievements provide no final goal" and that thus serves as "a reminder of our limits and an affirmation of our hope."[3]

Throughout the twentieth century, a strand of nonviolence developed that brought together the international peacemaking impulse of the social gospel movement with the sober realism of Niebuhr. As with Niebuhr, proponents of what we here call *realist nonviolence* hold up Jesus as the ultimate ethical ideal,

---

2. See, for example, Niebuhr, *Interpretation of Christian Ethics*.
3. Lovin, *Reinhold Niebuhr and Christian Realism*, 1; Lovin, *Christian Realism and the New Realities*, 1.

but they also concede, with Niebuhr, that moral dilemmas in this fallen world often require compromises of that ideal. The most that human societies can hope to accomplish is not the absolute perfection of Christ but rather an approximation of that ideal in the form of relative justice. Where nonviolent realists part from Niebuhr is over his insistence on the necessity of violence to establish this relative justice. For nonviolent realists, while some kind of minimal force may be necessary at times to establish justice, nonviolent peacemaking initiatives are almost always more effective than war in establishing justice.

In this chapter, we trace the lineage of realist nonviolence from the social gospel movement in the early twentieth century to its contemporary manifestation in the just peacemaking movement. We highlight the work of Baptist theologians Walter Rauschenbusch and Glen Stassen, Methodist theologian Georgia Harkness, Mennonite theologians J. Lawrence Burkholder and Duane K. Friesen, and Catholic ethicists Gerald Schlabach and Lisa Sowle Cahill. As we describe the common features of their approaches to nonviolence, we also highlight the particular contours of each of their respective approaches.

The Eschatological Ethics of Realist Nonviolence

Reinhold Niebuhr's Christian realism is often seen as marking a radical break from the social gospel movement that preceded it. But while he chastised the social gospel movement for its naive optimism that failed to account for human depravity, Niebuhr identifies Walter Rauschenbusch, a leading theologian of the social gospel, as "the voice of realism at the turn of the century."[4] As Niebuhr develops his social ethic in the years following the war, he acknowledges his own "general adhesion to

---

4. Niebuhr, "Walter Rauschenbusch in Historical Perspective," 34.

the purposes of the 'Social Gospel' of which Rauschenbusch was the most celebrated exponent."[5] Rauschenbusch himself describes the social gospel as "realistic in its interests," focusing on the concrete ethical aspects of Jesus's life and ministry over abstract metaphysical speculation about Jesus's natures.[6] Rauschenbusch argues that Jesus presents a number of "axiomatic social convictions" about the value of life, human solidarity, and standing up for the marginalized.[7] On the question of violence in particular, Rauschenbusch identifies Jesus as committed to absolute nonresistance, which he argues is not "a strange and erratic part of [Jesus's] teaching" but "an essential part of his conception of life and of his God-consciousness."[8] Nevertheless, Rauschenbusch does not naively suggest that societies should determine policy by asking, *What would Jesus do?*[9] Instead, Rauschenbusch argues that "the dominant purpose" of Jesus's life was "the establishment of the Kingdom of God."[10]

For Rauschenbusch, the kingdom of God is "an ideal human society, constituted according to divine laws and governed by God."[11] In Rauschenbusch's thought, the kingdom of God serves as an eschatological ideal that is never fully realizable

5. Niebuhr, *Interpretation of Christian Ethics*, 8. The complex relationship between Rauschenbusch's thought and Niebuhr's has been the subject of a number of studies over many decades. See Dickinson, "Rauschenbusch and Niebuhr"; Stackhouse, "Eschatology and Ethical Method"; Beckley, *Passion for Justice*; Robbins, *Methods in the Madness*; Evans, "Ties That Bind"; Cramer, "Theopolitics."

6. Rauschenbusch, *Theology for the Social Gospel*, 147. Rauschenbusch writes that the social gospel "may create a feeling of apathy toward speculative questions" since it is "modern and is out for realities. It is ethical and wants ethical results from theology" (148).

7. See Rauschenbusch, *Social Principles of Jesus*. The quotation comes from the title of part 1.

8. Rauschenbusch, *Theology for the Social Gospel*, 263.

9. This phrase was popularized by fellow social gospel proponent Charles Monroe Sheldon's bestselling novel, *In His Steps*.

10. Rauschenbusch, *Theology for the Social Gospel*, 150.

11. Rauschenbusch, *Righteousness of the Kingdom*, 98.

within history but that serves as a perpetual standard to strive for and to use to critique current social systems.[12] "At best there is always but an approximation to a perfect social order," Rauschenbusch writes. "The kingdom of God is always but coming."[13] This eschatological tension between the ideal of the kingdom and the realities of fallen societies—and the moral dilemmas and ambiguities this tension creates—would become a hallmark of Christian realism in both its non-pacifist and pacifist forms.

Rauschenbusch's own increasingly strident pacifism in the later years of his life was based not on optimism about human societies' ability to emulate Jesus but rather on a realistic assessment of the moral and political destructiveness of war. "The Great War has dwarfed and submerged all other issues, including our social problems," writes Rauschenbusch. "But in fact the war is the most acute and tremendous social problem of all."[14] For Rauschenbusch, the Great War revealed war itself to be "the supreme moral evil," "the supreme expression of hate and the completest cessation of freedom," and "a catastrophic stage in the coming of the Kingdom of God."[15] War is, in short, the greatest manifestation of the kingdom of Evil with which the kingdom of God is in conflict.[16] For nonviolent realists like Rauschenbusch, rejecting war is not a matter of optimism or perfectionism. Rather, it is based on a realistic recognition that

12. As Max Stackhouse explains, "The logic and structure of Rauschenbusch's thought about the Kingdom of God is precisely the same as that used to analyze and evaluate modern society. Indeed, it is the model upon which the evaluation is based. In so far as the social system lends itself to the development of the integrated structure which Rauschenbusch sets forth in the eschatological formulations, it is approved; in so far as it diverts or inhibits developments toward the Kingdom of God, it is criticized and radical transformation is called for." "Eschatology and Ethical Method," 81.

13. Rauschenbusch, *Christianity and the Social Crisis*, 338; cf. 251.

14. Rauschenbusch, *Theology for the Social Gospel*, 4.

15. Rauschenbusch, *Theology for the Social Gospel*, 35, 143, 226.

16. Rauschenbusch, *Theology for the Social Gospel*, 226.

war in no way approximates the ideals of the kingdom of God but is in direct opposition to them.[17]

In the aftermath of the Great War, a young Methodist philosopher named Georgia Harkness joined a young Reinhold Niebuhr and others on a trip to Europe led by social gospel evangelist Sherwood Eddy. While their firsthand encounters with survivors of the war and their observations of the war's destructiveness disabused both Harkness and Niebuhr of any lingering naive optimism they may have shared, they each drew differing lessons. Niebuhr came to reject the pacifism of the social gospel as naive and unrealistic, while Harkness came to adopt it as the only realistic way to pursue peace and justice in a fallen world. As Harkness later reflects, "My trip to Rheims and the battlefields, with what I saw in Germany of the effects of the hunger blockade and the 'war-peace,' have made me a pacifist, I think, forevermore."[18] Harkness eventually moved from teaching philosophy to teaching theology—becoming the first woman to teach theology at an American seminary and the first woman to be an elected member of the American Theological Society[19]—and she admits in a 1939 essay that wrestling with the thought of theologians like Niebuhr and Paul Tillich caused her earlier liberalism to become "chastened and deepened."[20] But, despite these changes, her pacifism remained consistent:

> I have become a more convinced pacifist in a day when many better Christians than I have felt impelled to surrender their pacifism. The reasons are both pragmatic and theological. War destroys every value for which Christianity stands, and

---

17. Rauschenbusch's major works have recently been re-released in three volumes as *Walter Rauschenbusch: Published Works and Selected Writings*.

18. Quoted in Keller, *Georgia Harkness*, 140.

19. See Micks, "Georgia Harkness," 311; Harkness, "Spiritual Pilgrimage," 348.

20. Harkness, "Spiritual Pilgrimage," 349.

to oppose war by more war is only to deepen the morass into which humanity has fallen. . . .

But deeper than this is the realism which has come with the shattering of whatever illusions our liberalism had. I believe that life is inevitably a sphere of conflict and that our choices are not often to be made between good and evil, but between alternative evils. I believe that in all of life's dark areas the triumph which shines through tragedy comes not with the sword which our Lord rejected, but with the cross toward which he walked. I believe that only in the union of justice with suffering love is any human force redemptive and permanently curative, for only in such union is force more than human.[21]

While Harkness cites the example of Jesus, she does not base her pacifism on strict observance of Jesus's teachings in the Gospels. Harkness agrees with Niebuhr that Jesus's ethic is "absolute" and says little about "the question of compromise in the practical affairs of the social, political, and economic orders, where any course that *can* be followed leads to unideal results below the standards of the Kingdom."[22] On the question of compromise, Harkness agrees with Niebuhr: "There is a place for compromise. The absolute demands of love must be lived out within the relativities of human existence in which duties come mixed, and a perfect course of action is seldom open to us." Harkness thus believes that coercive force is necessary to maintain "an approximation of justice," but she argues that physical force "should be used as little as possible, and always under constraint." Harkness advocates for the use of

21. Harkness, "Spiritual Pilgrimage," 350.
22. Harkness, *Christian Ethics*, 64. Cf. Harkness, *Sources of Western Morality*, 227: "Jesus made unqualified demands. He never watered down God's righteousness to easy human performance. To love one's enemies, for example, is no simple or natural achievement. How, then, gain the power? Jesus was apparently not concerned with the moral dilemma posed by what is now called perfectionism."

middle axioms as a way of commending an approximation of the ethic of Jesus in the political sphere. As she describes, "A middle axiom is not something of permanent validity, as the love commandment is, nor is it a specific legislative policy, but an intermediate guidepost derived from Christian ethics as to what must be done next. . . . Provided such middle axioms are taken for what they are, as Christian 'next steps' and not as a watered-down version of the full implications of the love commandment, they can be extremely helpful in the quest of a fuller justice as this is actuated by Christian love."[23]

While Niebuhr was critical of the liberal pacifism of the social gospel movement, he commended the apolitical nonresistance of Mennonites as being faithful to the teachings of Jesus, though he believed such nonresistance is only possible by disavowing "all responsibility for social justice."[24] This backhanded compliment did not sit well with more politically engaged Mennonites. During World War II, J. Lawrence Burkholder, then a young Mennonite pastor, was shaken by the dilemma of "either killing other human beings or letting Hitler kill with abandon."[25] He decided to take a third option, enlisting with Mennonite Central Committee to fly relief aid into war-torn China. However, as he later reflected, "the China years that followed became the crucible for my ethical thinking. I had never had a course in ethics; my ethics came directly out of the encounter between Mennonite radical idealism and reality."[26] Under the influence of the social gospel and Niebuhr (among others), Burkholder developed a

23. Harkness, *Christian Ethics*, 116, 191, 192, 190–91.
24. Niebuhr, "Why the Christian Church Is Not Pacifist," 30.
25. Burkholder, "Limits of Perfection," 5. A longer version of Burkholder's autobiography based on recorded interviews was published posthumously as Burkholder, *Recollections of a Sectarian Realist*.
26. Burkholder, "Limits of Perfection," 6.

Mennonite ethic of social responsibility, which acknowledges that "the clash between Christ's ethic and the facts of social existence [is] simply inescapable" and thereby gives greater appreciation for "structural ambiguity, power, moral conflict, institutional sin, and social responsibility."[27] However, while Burkholder makes room for moral dilemmas and compromises within his social ethic, as a pacifist he draws the line "at the point of killing human beings," arguing that "to kill a human being is to remove him or her from the realm of repentance, renewal, and salvation."[28]

As a fellow Mennonite realist, Duane K. Friesen shares Burkholder's general methodology—his "dialectic between faith and reason or experience"—but he faults Burkholder for uncritically adopting Niebuhr's view of Jesus as "'purely religious,' without any social ethic." For Friesen, this presents a docetic view of Jesus as disembodied and unconcerned with the political and social conditions of his day, a view that Friesen finds at odds with the New Testament picture of Jesus. At the same time, Friesen does not take the route of nonviolence of Christian discipleship that we discussed in chapter 1. He writes that "one cannot develop a Christian ethic simply by looking to Jesus"; instead, "a Christian social ethic must be grounded in a broader theological framework that includes doctrines of creation, sin, redemption, and eschatology, understood in the light of Jesus Christ." Regarding an ethic of the state, Friesen calls for the use of "middle axioms" that "bridge the gap between the church and political institutions," ultimately advocating for

27. Burkholder, *Mennonite Ethics*, 243; Burkholder, "How Do We Do Peace Theology?," 34. On his influences, see Burkholder, *Mennonite Ethics*, 209–14; Burkholder, "Concluding Postscript," 146. For Burkholder's views on social responsibility, see his published dissertation, *Problem of Social Responsibility*, reprinted in Burkholder, *Mennonite Ethics*.

28. Burkholder, "How Do We Do Peace Theology?," 33.

"nonviolent resolution of conflict" as the norm for the pacifist, as we discuss below.[29]

In sum, nonviolent realists agree with Niebuhr's general mode of ethical reasoning, but they stop short at the use of violence to establish relative justice. They do not claim to derive their nonviolence directly from Jesus's injunctions to "turn the other cheek" and "resist not evil." They do not deny that nonviolent resistance involves coercion and compromise. They do not claim to be free of self-regard and sin. Rather, as they attempt to approximate the ethic of Jesus with a full understanding of the realities of human sin—especially as it is manifested in geopolitical conflict—they simply argue that nonviolent approaches to conflict resolution are the most realistic and least destructive approaches available. This leads them to reject war and to seek nonviolent alternatives, a judgment based not on moral absolutes but on a realistic assessment of the facts.

The Empirical Basis of Realist Nonviolence

On July 8, 1915, while the United States officially remained neutral in the war in Europe, Rauschenbusch and Congregational minister Charles Aked coauthored the leaflet "Private Profit and the Nation's Honor: A Protest and a Plea," which condemned the shipment of arms and ammunition from US factories to Great Britain.[30] In their leaflet, they cut through the idealistic rhetoric of those praising the United States for

---

29. Friesen, "On Doing Social Ethics," 129, 131, 132, 132–33.

30. Rauschenbusch and Aked, "Private Profit and the Nation's Honor." The leaflet concludes with these lines: "The material is released to the press. We shall welcome the aid of anyone who will give publicity to this protest by publishing, reprinting, quoting or discussing it. Let every man consider whether his hands are stained by this traffic, and what he has done to cleanse them." For a discussion of this piece, see Evans, *Kingdom Is Always but Coming*, 267–68. For the full text, see https://www.patheos.com/blogs/anabaptistrevisions/2020/01/private-profit-nations-honor.

staying out of the war. Instead, they follow the money: "The Christian sentiment of our people has taken high moral ground on the war questions. We have pitied the European nations for their bleeding desolation. We have lectured them on their madness. We have solemnly met, at the call of our President, and prayed Almighty God to end the war. But when lucrative contracts came our way, a tremor of cupidity ran through financial circles, certain stocks went up by leaps and bounds, and the vast social resources of America turned around to feed and stoke the fires of destruction." For Rauschenbusch and Aked, staying out of the war did not make a nation peaceful, just as espousing pacifism did not remove one's complicity in violence. "In common with all other citizens of the United States we are morally involved in the trade in arms and ammunition," they write. "We wish to cleanse our conscience, at least, by protest."[31]

Rauschenbusch and Aked's leaflet illustrates a second feature of realist nonviolence: its empirical basis. Nonviolent realists argue that, in order to choose the course of action most likely to approximate the ideals of the kingdom in a given context, one must first have a realistic assessment of the facts on the ground. With a realistic awareness of the human condition, they reject the idealistic pretensions of both absolute pacifists and those who believe that peace can be achieved by winning a war. As Harkness writes, a requirement for establishing justice is "intelligent analysis of the situation, knowledge of the facts, clear-seeing judgment of the circumstances and of the most feasible methods of changing them for the better. In projects calling for action, one must look before he leaps."[32]

Friesen concedes that "the most serious weakness in pacifist literature is its failure to connect a theological and ethical

---

31. Rauschenbusch and Aked, "Private Profit and the Nation's Honor."
32. Harkness, *Ministry of Reconciliation*, 107.

framework with an empirical understanding of the world of international politics," a weakness that he seeks to remedy by "attending to relevant research from the social sciences concerning international politics."[33] Thus, while Friesen agrees with all realists on the pervasiveness of human sinfulness, he tests the assumption that collective human sinfulness necessarily manifests itself in the form of war. According to Friesen, certain expressions of human sinfulness occur under certain conditions but not under others. The goal for the nonviolent realist is to isolate the conditions in which human sinfulness expresses itself in war and then to attempt to change those conditions.[34]

The Ecumenical Potential of Realist Nonviolence

Shortly after the end of the Cold War and the collapse of the Soviet Union in the early 1990s, Baptist theologian Glen Stassen began to articulate a form of realist nonviolence that he named "just peacemaking," a tertium quid between pacifism and just war. Viewing the Sermon on the Mount not as a series of perfectionist statements but as a series of "transforming initiatives," Stassen proposes that the way forward with respect to peacemaking lies in viewing it as a proactive movement rather than a reactive one. While Stassen's approach is more directly based on Jesus's teachings than are the approaches of other figures discussed in this chapter, he acknowledges that his thought is also rooted in the Christian realism of his Union Theological Seminary teacher Reinhold Niebuhr. In particular, he credits Niebuhr with teaching him "to pay attention less to the hopeful ideals people declare than to their basic interests, loyalties,

---

33. Friesen, *Christian Peacemaking and International Conflict*, 29.
34. For a similar argument from a Catholic perspective, see Cochran, *Catholic Realism and the Abolition of War*.

and power relations, and less to the promises of their high-sounding words than to the pattern of their actions." Stassen thus criticizes Niebuhr "not for his realism but for his missing the delivering dimensions of Jesus' ethic."[35]

Instead of viewing war as a problem to be addressed when it erupts, just peacemaking emphasizes a series of peacemaking initiatives at both interpersonal and international levels. The seven practices of Stassen's initial volume were later expanded into ten practices, including everything from advancing democracy and human rights to reducing offensive weapons trade. In Stassen's vision, nonviolence stands as one practice among others—and often in direct tension with other practices. For example, nonviolent direct action is included alongside the reduction of weapons sales, though, unlike the former, the latter does not call for nations to lay down their arms entirely.[36]

One of the practical advantages of just peacemaking, for Stassen, is that one need not be a committed pacifist in order to engage in peacemaking initiatives. Because the initiatives are rooted not only in Jesus's teaching but also in an empirical, data-driven analysis of the causes of violence and the most effective means of reducing it, they have the potential to bring together both pacifists and advocates of just war theory. This provides ecumenical possibilities for just peacemaking, as theological debates between just war traditions and pacifist ones are sidelined in favor of practical alliances.

Theologian and ethicist Gerald Schlabach, a self-declared Mennonite Catholic, sees in just peacemaking a "remarkable historical convergence" between pacifists and just war

---

35. Stassen, *Just Peacemaking: Transforming Initiatives*, 53–88, 14–15, 60.

36. Stassen, *Just Peacemaking: Transforming Initiatives*, 53–88, 14–15, 60. See also Stassen, *Just Peacemaking: Ten Practices*. For appreciative criticisms of Stassen's work, see Werntz, "War in Christ's World," 90–96; Scheid, *Just Revolution*, 28–32; Stone, "Realist Criticism of Just Peacemaking," 255–67.

advocates. "Prominent examples are the Roman Catholic Church," he writes, "which has long been custodian of the just war tradition, as well as Protestant ecumenical representatives who gathered with others to work carefully on initiatives such as the Just Peacemaking project of the 1990s, and historic peace churches such as Mennonites." While Schlabach acknowledges that there may never be complete theological convergence, he believes that in just peacemaking "it is now possible to imagine that war, at least, might cease to be a church-dividing issue."[37]

In order to bring pacifist and just war advocates together for the common cause of eliminating war, Schlabach proposes shifting the paradigm to what he calls "just policing." He explains, "What 'just policing' especially highlights is twofold: If the best intentions of the just war theorists were operational, they could only allow for just policing, not warfare at all. If Christian pacifists can in any way support, participate [in], or at least not object to operations with recourse to limited but potentially lethal force, that will only be true for just policing."[38] Schlabach believes that a just policing paradigm leads each tradition to focus on embodying the best concrete practices of their respective tradition instead of focusing on disembodied theoretical debates about violence.[39]

As with Schlabach, Catholic ethicist Lisa Sowle Cahill also calls both just war advocates and pacifists to "yield to the more pragmatic, realistic, and appropriately ambiguous work that is

37. Schlabach, "Just Policing and the Christian Call to Nonviolence," 405.

38. Schlabach, "Just Policing and the Christian Call to Nonviolence," 407. See also Schlabach, *Just Policing, Not War.*

39. The just policing paradigm has received criticism for painting too idealistic a picture of police action, especially when racial dynamics of policing are taken into consideration. See Alexis-Baker, "Gospel or a Glock?" An entire issue of the *Conrad Grebel Review* (Spring 2008) was devoted to this debate. See especially Schlabach, "Just the Police Function, Then"; Alexis-Baker, "Community, Policing, and Violence." See also Schlabach, "Must Christian Pacifists Reject Police Force?"

peacebuilding." In chapter 2 we discussed Cahill and her 1994 work, *Love Your Enemies*, which presents a more ecclesiocentric, virtue-based approach to nonviolence. However, more recently Cahill revisited her earlier work in light of developments in just peacemaking from Stassen and others and published a significant update as *Blessed Are the Peacemakers*, where she now advocates Christian peacebuilding as the approach that "best represents the Christian commitment both to nonviolence and to political responsibility."[40]

For Cahill, peacebuilding brings together the best insights of Protestant thinkers Dietrich Bonhoeffer and Reinhold Niebuhr with Catholic Social Teaching and the pacifism of Catholic activist Dorothy Day. As Cahill draws together insights from these thinkers and her own engagement with peacemaking theory and practice, she identifies six dimensions of peacebuilding in both its domestic and international forms. These include peacebuilding's effectiveness, the essential role women play in peacebuilding, and the necessity of "intercultural and interreligious cooperation" for peacebuilding.[41]

Conclusion

In the popular imagination, Christian nonviolence is often equated with what we described in chapter 1 as nonviolence of Christian discipleship. However, within the discipline of peace studies, realist nonviolence has grown over the last half century from a minority stream to arguably the predominant stream of Christian nonviolence within the academy today.[42] This development is due no doubt to the empirical, practical,

40. Cahill, *Blessed Are the Peacemakers*, viii, ix. See also Cahill, "Theology for Peacebuilding."

41. Cahill, *Blessed Are the Peacemakers*, 360. See also 325–60.

42. This is true even of Mennonites. See Driedger and Kraybill, *Mennonite Peacemaking*.

and ecumenical orientation of realist nonviolence—as peace studies has expanded beyond theology and biblical studies to include a wide array of disciplines and methodologies. This development is perhaps nowhere better seen than in the establishment of the Kroc Institute for International Peace Studies at the University of Notre Dame in South Bend, Indiana, in 1985, and the Center for Justice and Peacebuilding at Eastern Mennonite University in Harrisonburg, Virginia, a decade later.

A significant figure in this development is John Paul Lederach, who served as founding director of the Center for Justice and Peacebuilding in the mid-1990s before moving in 1999 to the Kroc Institute, where he continues to teach. Unlike earlier generations of realists—both pacifist and non-pacifist—who focused on state actors and thereby perpetuated Western imperialism, colonialism, and hegemony in the name of peacemaking, Lederach advocates a "grounded realism and constructive pessimism," which holds that genuine, constructive change can only occur when peacebuilding at national and international levels is connected organically to local communities at the level where violence occurred. Lederach puts little faith in peace accords that are not connected to every level of society in a complex relational web. Thus, instead of a top-down approach to peacebuilding, Lederach offers the image of "web making." He writes that "constructive change, perhaps more than anything else, is the art of strategically and imaginatively weaving relational webs across social spaces within settings of protracted violent conflict."[43]

Likewise, peacebuilding scholar and practitioner Janna Hunter-Bowman argues that, in contrast to "post-accord peacebuilding literatures" that "remain dominated by state-oriented

---

43. Lederach, *Moral Imagination*, 58, 78, 84. See also Lederach, *Building Peace*; Lederach, *Preparing for Peace*.

paradigms associated with the liberal peace," peacebuilding aimed at creating the conditions for authentic "justpeace" must "account for the ways grass-roots organizing, and broad-based social movements provide the foundation for [comprehensive peace agreements] and contribute to post-accord nation-building."[44] For Hunter-Bowman, the work of social transformation begins and ends with those most affected by violence—those she calls "agents under duress." Realistic peacebuilding therefore "decenters state institutions and lifts up grassroots participation" in ways that allow those most affected by violence to point the way to what is needed to transform institutions—including the state—to bring about authentic, lasting peace.[45] This turn to the voices and experiences of those most affected by violence and oppression connects realist nonviolence with the remaining forms of nonviolence and antiviolence that we take up in this book—streams arising from the Black church in the United States, impoverished and oppressed people of Latin America, and victim-survivors of sexual and gender-based violence around the world.

44. Hunter-Bowman, "Peace through Participation," 68.
45. Hunter-Bowman, "Constructive Agents under Duress," 149.

Nonviolence as Political Practice

BRINGING NONVIOLENCE INTO THE PUBLIC SQUARE

Sitting in Birmingham City Jail in 1963, Martin Luther King Jr. wrote a letter to his fellow clergy, answering their question as to why an "outside agitator" was leading the African American community of Birmingham, Alabama, in nonviolent protest. Acknowledging their complaint, he writes, "You deplore the demonstrations taking place in Birmingham. But your statement, I am sorry to say, fails to express a similar concern for the conditions that brought about the demonstrations. . . . It is unfortunate that demonstrations are taking place in Birmingham, but it is even more unfortunate that the city's white power structure left the Negro community with no alternative." It was not, we assume, the virtue of nonviolence or peacefulness of heart that proved troublesome to the white ministers of Birmingham. Rather, it was the public protest that embodied these virtues. King assures them that for him this is a false dichotomy, emphasizing the discipline and "self-purification" that the demonstrators had undergone to prepare hearts, consciences, and bodies for the difficulties ahead. But the exchange is telling, for it signals the emergence of a different way of thinking about Christian nonviolence as not just a private virtue but also a public, political action.[1]

King was not the first to organize mass nonviolent protests; theologically generated nonviolent protest had long been a part of the Christian repertoire, particularly in North America.[2] But the witness of King and many others in the civil rights movement opened up the imaginative possibilities for nonviolence as a political act, as the movement gained the attention of a broader US and worldwide audience.[3] One of the lingering questions that had dogged Christian nonviolence for decades, if not centuries, is what value it has for public life. As we saw in the last chapter, Reinhold Niebuhr gave prominent voice to this question. As he writes, "The pacifists do not know human nature well enough to be concerned about the contradictions between the law of love and the sin of man, until sin has conceived and brought forth death. They do not see that sin involves an element of conflict into the world and that even the most loving

1. King, "Letter from Birmingham Jail," 128, 129, 129–30.

2. For an overview of these pre–World War II precedents, see Brock, *Pacifism in the United States*, and Brock, *Pacifism in Europe to 1914*. Brock's numerous works on this topic are among the most essential sources available for cataloging the varieties of religious and secular forms of nonviolence.

3. The danger of focusing on King—the best-known and most prolific figure of the civil rights movement—is that it obscures the important nonviolent witness of many other figures. Other significant articulations of nonviolence from this era include Holsaert et al., *Hands on the Freedom Plow*; Young, *Easy Burden*; Roberts, *Liberation and Reconciliation*; and Hamer, *Speeches of Fannie Lou Hamer*. As a political scientist, Gene Sharp developed nonviolence as political practice throughout the latter half of the twentieth century and into the first part of the twenty-first, especially through his work at the Albert Einstein Institution, which he founded in 1983 to study forms of nonviolent activism and their efficacy. Since we focus on explicitly Christian forms of nonviolence, we do not discuss his work at length here. For more on Sharp and his approach to nonviolence, see the Albert Einstein Institution (www .aeinstein.org). See also Sharp's *Politics of Nonviolent Action* trilogy.

relations are not free of it."[4] Christian nonviolence, according to Niebuhr, deals naively with human nature and thus is unable to offer anything to the world of conflict. If Christian nonviolence speaks of a more perfect way of human relations, it remains nothing more than an ideal that we will always fall short of.[5] In the last chapter, we explored a stream of Christian nonviolence that takes up Niebuhr's challenge on its own terms. In this chapter, we explore another answer to Niebuhr's challenge: *nonviolence as political practice*. In contrast to other varieties, this stream of nonviolence is not as concerned with how nonviolence is practicable as a Christian discipline or how it is consistent with Christian virtue; instead, this stream is primarily concerned with how nonviolence—as a normative Christian practice—can be the basis for public action.

The Roots of Nonviolent Political Practice

Christian nonviolence first occurred not as a practical teaching but as the logical outworking of a Christian commitment.[6] Early Christians' first question was not whether nonviolence could be applied as a political commitment within the public realm but whether participation in war and celebrating other forms of public violence such as gladiatorial contests were consistent with the

4. Niebuhr, "Why the Christian Church Is Not Pacifist," 35.

5. For Niebuhr, unrealizable ideals remained helpful, in that they critique our actions and remind us of our sinful shortcomings, but political application of nonviolence is "morally absurd." See Niebuhr, "Why the Christian Church Is Not Pacifist," 32–33.

6. Discussion of the degree to which early Christians adopted an ethic of nonviolence and their reasons for doing so is beyond the scope of this book. In *Caesar and the Lamb*, George Kalantzis argues that nonviolence was unambiguously accepted. This counters older arguments for ambiguity within the earliest sources, such as Helgeland, Daly, and Burns, *Christians and the Military*; Harnack, *Militia Christi*; and Swift, *Early Fathers on War and Military Service*. In *Soldiering for God*, John F. Shean takes a middle position, arguing that the opinions of Christian leaders on this point did not speak universally for the laity (105–77).

Christian life. The evolution of Christian nonviolence from an internal commitment to an outward political ethic was a much later development. Between the patristic era and the nineteenth century, there were a number of times when an internal Christian movement provided the basis and pattern for action within the public body politic. The Peace of God, the Truce of God, and the establishment of Pennsylvania are three early examples.[7]

As we saw in the last chapter, the nineteenth century brought with it the establishment of peace societies both in Europe and in North America, composed of broad coalitions of both Christians and non-Christians who opposed war for religious and practical reasons. Though rooted in Christian practice, groups such as the American Peace Society (APS) in North America and the *Société de la paix de Genève* (Geneva Peace Society) were, in the words of APS founder William Ladd, concerned with "organization above purification."[8] Between the late 1800s and the end of World War I, a variety of movements, such as the 1899 Hague Peace Conference, sought to put into practice bilateral agreements, legal frameworks, and processes of de-escalation designed to rule out war. Movements such as the Peace Ballot campaign in Britain, a pragmatic pacifist movement, garnered nearly a million supporters by 1935.[9] These early pragmatic peace movements were cast as isolationist and accused of appeasing tyrants in the wake of World War I and World War II, as those committed to conflict resolution by legal means instead of physical violence also broadly refused military service.[10] But in the decades following World War II,

7. Head, "Development of the Peace of God," 656–86; Firnhaber-Baker, "From God's Peace to the King's Order," 19–30; Hershberger, "Pacifism and the State in Colonial Pennsylvania," 54–74.

8. Quoted in Cortright, *Peace*, 28.

9. Cortright, *Peace*, 76–77.

10. Cortright, *Peace*, 89.

nonviolence as political practice proliferated in a variety of forms. Proponents of this form of nonviolence began to focus on practical ways to confront war, including opposition to nuclear testing and the draft. Japan even went so far as to enshrine nonviolence in its constitution.[11]

Among Christians, nonviolence as political practice became enshrined in both international and domestic forms. In its international form, as seen in Christian Peacemaker Teams, nonviolent direct action takes the form of mediation between warring factions and proactively pursuing de-escalation of conflict.[12] Although it tends to operate from below instead of at the level of geopolitics, this form has many parallels with the realist nonviolence discussed in the last chapter and so will not be our primary focus here. Instead, our primary focus for this chapter is the domestic form—as seen in the American civil rights movement of the 1950s and 1960s and in the South African democratic struggles of the 1980s—in which direct action became the preferred mode of engagement. Far from designating a withdrawal from society, nonviolent direct action confronted injustice and conflict via demonstrations, protests, and other forms of public performance.[13]

As Christians began to articulate a version of nonviolence that is oriented toward public practice, three aspects of its practice emerged, aspects that will frame the remainder of this chapter. First, as with realist nonviolence, nonviolence as political practice coheres to empirically driven insights about the nature of conflict. Second, Christian nonviolence functions as a practice that is oriented toward the common good, enabling

11. Katz, *Ban the Bomb*; Rohr, *Prophets without Honor*; Moskos and Chambers, *New Conscientious Objectors*; Cortright, *Peace*, 120–21.

12. Sider, *Nonviolent Action*, 141–54.

13. For an account of this transition, using the Fellowship of Reconciliation as a case study, see Kosek, *Acts of Conscience*.

a society to flourish and conflicts to be resolved. Third, because of these first two insights, Christian thought and practices may be motivations for political nonviolence, but ultimately they point practitioners toward public and nonsectarian forms of action. This final point is a practical recognition but also leads to interfaith conclusions: nonviolent political practice bears witness to the God of creation, who is recognized by many names by adherents to various faith traditions.

Christian Nonviolence and Natural Law

Arguments for nonviolence as political practice include appeals to faith commitments but typically focus on publicly available empirical grounds. According to this approach, the natural law argument for Christian nonviolence is proven by the workability of political nonviolence. The empirical arguments of this kind have been discussed with respect to realist nonviolence and will not be rehearsed here, but what differentiates this variety of Christian nonviolence is the commitment to nonviolence as a practice consistent with the deepest theologic of the created order. Long before popular movements of the twentieth century gave empirical credence to religiously inspired political nonviolence, proponents of strategic nonviolence had been making the argument that nonviolence speaks to the truest aspects of the created order.[14] Long-time secretary of the Fellowship of Reconciliation, A. J. Muste, in his work *Of Holy Disobedience*, argues that the everyday is the space within which people render service to God; as such, the "order of redemption" that Christians talk about is seen in the vocation to resist conscription and to not cooperate

14. For a discussion of the natural law presuppositions of Christian nonviolence, see Hauerwas, *With the Grain of the Universe*.

with the wars of governments.[15] The call of God appears not in the mystical but in the ordinary participation of the peaceable ordering of the world; in these acts of conscience, Muste argues, there is no Jew or gentile, as both are participating in a "holy disobedience" against a new Caesar.[16] As a Quaker, Muste held that the natural law of God is manifest whenever people take up democratic ideals in a peaceable manner, where "the Spirit has so often whispered in the inner chambers of man's soul: Renounce violence."[17]

The appeal to natural law categories for Christian political nonviolence is not restricted to Quakers, who have emphasized the dignity of all persons and the movement of God in various guises.[18] King's well-known dictum, "The moral arc of the universe is long, but it bends toward justice," operates in this way as well.[19] His personalism—the belief that God is interested in us as human persons and that through our personhood we understand how God invites us to see the universe as built on moral principles in which all persons have God-given dignity—requires a form of social witness (nonviolence) that comports with the natural laws of the world as ordained by God.[20] Dorothy Day likewise held that the natural law, which culminates in the person of Christ, demands nonviolence in the face of conflict.[21] In Pope Francis's recent World Day of Peace

15. Muste, *Of Holy Disobedience*, 12–13.

16. Muste, *Of Holy Disobedience*, 24, 30.

17. Muste, *Nonviolence in an Aggressive World*, 9. As Muste describes, the natural grain of nonviolence leads to a political program of nonviolence (132–72). For a fuller theological exposition of this theme, see Muste, *Not by Might*.

18. See Dandelion, *Quakers*.

19. King, *Testament of Hope*, 277. King is here appropriating the language of nineteenth-century Unitarian minister and abolitionist Theodore Parker. See Insko, *History, Abolition*, 212.

20. Baldwin, "Rufus Burrow"; Burrow, *God and Human Dignity*. Thanks to Malinda Elizabeth Berry for this way of describing personalism.

21. Werntz, *Bodies of Peace*, 132–37. On the use of natural law in arguments for nonviolence, see Martens, "With the Grain of the Universe."

message, he lauds the empirical practicality of nonviolence, while also emphasizing the correspondence of nonviolence to divine grace. Worked out in practice, nonviolence, for Francis, is the fruit of the nucleus of human life—the rightly ordered family—radiating out into all society.[22]

Christian Nonviolence and the Public Square

While Christian nonviolence as political practice has a number of religious roots and precedents—the early church, the sixteenth-century Radical Reformers, the Quakers, and so on—its direct twentieth-century influences come from two sources outside the Christian tradition: Gandhi and the insurgent labor movements of the early twentieth century. Whereas Gandhi directly influenced figures such as King, Desmond Tutu, and César Chávez, the work of the socialist groups such as the Industrial Workers of the World (or the "Wobblies") became an organizing influence of earlier public forms of Christian nonviolence.[23] The Wobblies linked international war with domestic forms of violence against the working class, such that war was of the same genus as unjust labor practices, grouped under the rubric of "violence." Groups such as the Fellowship of Reconciliation, a group that grew from Quaker roots, had connected these issues in their advocacy before King's famous "Beyond Vietnam" speech.[24] While such figures and groups sometimes perceive the overlap between domestic and international forms of violence, most advocates of political nonviolence tend to focus on either domestic or international applications of Christian nonviolence.

22. Francis, "Nonviolence," §5. We discuss both Day and Francis at greater length in chapter 2 above.

23. Kosek, *Acts of Conscience*, 41–48.

24. For background on the Fellowship of Reconciliation (FOR), see Dekar, *Creating the Beloved Community*. For a more critical take on the FOR and three other related groups, see Lewy, *Peace and Revolution*.

Domestic forms of nonviolence take multiple forms—protests, strikes, and other forms of noncompliance—and broadly have the goal of persuasion. Richard Gregg, one of the early American proponents of nonviolence, refers to this tactical movement as "moral jujitsu." Nonviolence is by definition in a physically weaker position. By not resorting to instruments of violence but by using its weakness in order to persuade, nonviolent forms of demonstration use the stronger party's force against them as a source of shame.[25]

Christian proponents who emphasize domestic uses of nonviolence agree on the practicality of nonviolence, but their work frequently builds on a moral universe that is shared with their opponents. For this reason King, for example, emphasized the role of nonviolence as pricking the American conscience. King describes mass civil disobedience as "a strategy for social change which is at least as forceful as an ambulance with its siren on full." Articulating the goal of such protests by the civil rights movement as "creat[ing] a crisis the nation couldn't ignore," King intended to use nonviolence both to draw attention to racial injustice and to persuade and convict the conscience of their opposition.[26] Various tactics can be used in service to this end, but domestic tactics served the ends of publicizing immoral actions and putting pressure on white consciences with respect to racial injustices. Others, such as J. Deotis Roberts, emphasize the practical peacebuilding

25. Gregg, *Power of Nonviolence*. As we mention above, this more pragmatic approach was adopted and refined in the secular realm by Gene Sharp, who in numerous works treats nonviolence as a tactical approach designed to minimize bloodshed and facilitate democratic participation. See, in particular, Sharp's trilogy, *Politics of Nonviolent Action*. Not all proponents of political nonviolence would agree with Gregg that nonviolence is, indeed, the weaker position, nor would all agree that shaming is itself nonviolent since it could do moral harm to one's opponent, as the term *moral jujitsu* suggests. Thanks to Malinda Elizabeth Berry for these observations about Gregg's approach.

26. King, "Revolution of Nonviolent Resistance," 148–49.

aspects of political nonviolence as well. In exercising protest in a nonviolent fashion, the civil rights movement provided opportunity for interracial and democratic coalitions to be built. But this practical emphasis is built on a theological conviction that "the one who liberates reconciles, and the one who reconciles liberates." Black theologies of liberation, for Roberts, need not necessitate violence in the pursuit of liberation but emphasize that Black persons have a Christ-given dignity that bears itself out in nonviolent action that seeks reconciliation with white persons who seek to cause them harm.[27]

For those who view Christian nonviolence as political practice, the Scriptures that justify and motivate Christians toward nonviolence are not simply for liturgical use but provide a basis for public, democratic behavior. The Plowshares movement, best known for its public demonstrations against nuclear armament, would often incorporate Scripture into their ceremonial acts. In 2002, three Dominican sisters enacted the vision of Isaiah 2:4 by climbing into a nuclear silo site, striking the silos with hammers, and pouring blood on the grounds.[28] The Plowshares movement, begun in the wake of similar protests during the Vietnam War era and led in part by Catholic priests Daniel and Philip Berrigan, emphasizes the public performance of nonviolence as both prophetic criticism and public speech.[29] Because nonviolence of this form—for example, protesting a nuclear facility—can be understood by both a religious and a nonreligious audience, distinctively Christian acts enter the public square without losing their specifically Christian

27. Roberts, *Liberation and Reconciliation*, 20, 102–7.

28. Recounted in Nepstad, *Religion and War Resistance in the Plowshares Movement*, 1.

29. For an account of the Berrigans' witness in this way, see Stringfellow and Towne, *Suspect Tenderness*. We discuss the Berrigan brothers and the Plowshares movement at greater length in chapter 4 on apocalyptic nonviolence.

orientation, and they retain an additional depth of meaning for the Christians involved.

Whereas apocalyptic nonviolence views the intended purpose of nonviolent public acts as a way of bearing witness and realist nonviolence focuses on the political effectiveness of such actions, nonviolence as political practice views this distinction as a false dichotomy. Both those who advocate nonviolent strikes and those who, like the Dominican sisters, symbolically enact their nonviolent protests are committed to the public performance of nonviolence, regardless of the outcome. The commitment to Christian nonviolence as political practice is not a precursor to other possible forms of engagement but is intrinsic to a Christian witness against social injustice.

Interreligious Implications of Political Nonviolence

As we saw with the nonviolent mystics, communion with God calls forth an intimate connection between the being of God and the act of nonviolence. This connection between God's nature and the act of nonviolence is not limited to the mystics, as it can also be found among proponents of nonviolence of Christian discipleship. Political nonviolence differs from these other streams not with respect to God calling forth nonviolence but with respect to the application and audience of such an action.

Much political nonviolence in the twentieth century, both of Christian and non-Christian varieties, was linked with democratic aspirations.[30] In the cases of popular uprisings in Iran, the Philippines, and Poland, for example, autocratic or Communist governments were overthrown through mass nonviolent

---

30. As Nepstad observes in *Nonviolent Revolutions*, xiv–xv, democratic outcomes do not always result from nonviolent uprisings, nor are they always desired by the participants.

protests in pursuit of a more democratic alternative.[31] Nonviolence, as an ethos that rejects the silencing of minority voices within a body politic, has gone imaginatively hand in hand with a democratic politic in which multiple voices can be recognized.[32] The marriage of democratic politics with Christian nonviolence is thus a movement away from absolutist nonresistance, as democracy at its best—both in protest and in its normal processes—is a kind of coercion that sits uncomfortably with traditional commitments to nonresistance.

The democratic orientation of political nonviolence lends to its practitioners seeking common cause from a plural audience. In the career of King, for example, multiple kinds of public performances appear. At the onset of his career, explicitly theological actions accompanied the performance of nonviolence; the 1957 Prayer Pilgrimage to Washington, DC, which drew over thirty thousand participants, and the framing of Southern Christian Leadership Conference (SCLC) marches with Black spirituals are two examples of public nonviolence performed as an explicitly Christian act.[33] Other actions led by King, however, are more broadly performed. In these cases, King mobilizes the language of the church, though the performance is less explicitly religious in nature.[34] Vincent Lloyd, in his study of King, identifies this as a kind of natural law, albeit not an explicitly Christian one. Sometimes, such as in his "Letter from Birmingham Jail," King appeals to the Christian tradition of natural law in his opposition to segregation. But,

31. For analysis of these cases, see Chenoweth and Stephan, *Why Civil Resistance Works*.

32. Kosek, *Acts of Conscience*, details the ways Christian political nonviolence has been intertwined with democratic aspirations, both in theory and in practice.

33. Colaiaco, *Martin Luther King, Jr.*, 27, 61. For an excellent account of lay participation and visions of Christian nonviolence in the civil rights movement, see Holsaert et al., *Hands on the Freedom Plow*.

34. See Selby, *Martin Luther King and the Rhetoric of Freedom*.

as Lloyd argues, King's natural law is more anthropological and nonsectarian in nature. Nonviolence, seen in both the Hindu Gandhi and the Christian Black church, ultimately reflects an emotionally and practically accessible natural law that transcends religious affiliation.[35]

Similarly, among those who consider public performance to be the primary facet of Christian nonviolence, the viability and successes of political nonviolence bear witness to its theological validity as that which comports to the natural law, even if not performed by Christians. Occasionally, this is an implicit affirmation. In Ronald J. Sider's account of political nonviolence in the twentieth century, for example, Hindu, Muslim, and Christian "peace brigades" all speak of the same truth: nonviolent intervention in conflict works. Sider makes no effort to distinguish among the theological imports of these groups, but in some ways this is true to the genealogy of political nonviolence. After all, King's own form of nonviolence combined political tactics and spiritual self-discipline learned from Gandhi. Similarly, as Sider recounts, successful nonviolent revolts in East Germany and Poland are ecumenical nonviolent efforts in which churches participate but are not the primary participants.[36]

In domestic performances of nonviolence, the approaches of César Chávez and Desmond Tutu likewise bear out this nonsectarian vision of Christian nonviolence. Chávez, the leader of the United Farm Workers strikes, intentionally used a mixture of Catholic, Mexican, and democratic imagery in his strikes and protests. Speaking to one chronicler of the movement, Chávez notes, "For me, Christianity happens to be *a* natural *source of faith*. I have read what Christ said when he was here. He was

---

35. Lloyd, *Black Natural Law*, 88–117. See also Burrow, *God and Human Dignity*.
36. Sider, *Nonviolent Action*, 79–100. For an overview of King's relation to Gandhian practice and philosophy, see Burrow, *Extremist for Love*, 221–81, and King, "Pilgrimage to Nonviolence."

very clear in what he meant and knew exactly what he sought after." This broad appeal, by one chronicler's evaluation, was designed to connect to a Mesoamerican ethic of suffering that transcended religious confessionalism. Chávez's prayer that God would help this movement "to be human" speaks to this nexus of overlapping concerns—someone could be drawn to Chávez's movement without being Catholic, committed on the basis of their common political cause.[37]

Tutu, Nobel Laureate and Anglican archbishop working in the South African context of apartheid, likewise sees Jesus's work as nonsectarian. Commenting on the disunity in South Africa, he writes, "We have heard of God's dream from His prophets throughout history and modern times from great leaders and humanitarians like Martin Luther King, Jr., and Mahatma Gandhi. . . . The visions and triumphs of these prophets of God helped change their nations and inspire the rest of us around the world in our own struggles for equality."[38]

For Tutu, as with King, "it is a moral universe that we inhabit, and good and right and equity matter in the universe of the God we worship." Detailing the ways South Africans nonviolently and peacefully protested, Tutu distinguishes this approach from the violence emerging from within South African protests, writing that "in dehumanizing others, they are themselves dehumanized." By contrast, Tutu claims, "God created us for fellowship. God created us so that we should form the human family, existing together because we are made for one another." With the broader contours of society designated as the object for specifically religious protest, Tutu seeks to incorporate all

37. León, *Political Spirituality of Cesar Chavez*, 57–59, 67, 68. This overlapping political-spiritual interpretation of Chávez is in contrast to Orosco, *Cesar Chavez and the Common Sense of Nonviolence*, which emphasizes the public, democratic reason of Chávez, in which religion is translated into democratic idioms.

38. Tutu, *God Has a Dream*, 21–22.

persons, regardless of faith, into a common vision of political life inspired by the person of Jesus.[39] Michael Battle has described this as Tutu's "Ubuntu" theology, which begins with a doctrine of God rather than Christ. In this way, all people are seen as created in the image of God, prior to their religious affiliation or racial designation. Such a theological presupposition allows for divisive political constructions such as apartheid to be named as theological nonsense and for public reconciliation movements to reflect the deepest theological reality.[40]

Conclusion

Nonviolence as political practice, one of the best-known varieties of Christian nonviolence following the civil rights movement, comes with both liabilities and advantages. Nonviolent direct action seems in tension with some of Jesus's teachings, which seem to counsel nonresistance rather than nonviolent resistance. It becomes difficult to square Jesus's injunction to "resist not an evildoer" with forms of nonviolence that emphasize persuasion or nonviolent coercion, for example. Glen Stassen's commentary on the Sermon on the Mount—viewing the Sermon as a series of transformative initiatives—moves us part of the way toward reconciling this distance, but it does not likewise account for New Testament injunctions for the Christian to bear up under suffering rather than to directly oppose the force of evil.[41] These hermeneutical difficulties are surmountable but should be acknowledged.

Nonviolence as political practice has a similar impetus to realist nonviolence, but it is not willing to make nonviolence

---

39. Tutu, *Nobel Peace Prize Lecture*, 33, 38.

40. Battle, *Reconciliation*. For a comparison to King in particular, see Hill, *Theology of Martin Luther King, Jr. and Desmond Mpilo Tutu*.

41. Stassen, *Living the Sermon on the Mount*.

negotiable.[42] Trusting in the moral arc of the universe to bend, in God's providence, toward a justly ordered world, practitioners of Christian political nonviolence emphasize that means and ends must cohere: we cannot bear witness to an order characterized by nonviolence using violent means. This does not mean that adherents to political nonviolence follow the arguments of the mystics or of those who see nonviolence as intrinsic to Christian discipleship. As we have seen in this chapter, nonviolence as political practice trades on a much more public understanding of theology than either of those streams tend to. As such, while there may be overlap theologically, as in King's writing, between nonviolence of Christian discipleship and political forms of nonviolence, the mode of expression differs. For the figures discussed in this chapter, churches are involved with public nonviolent movements, but the primary interest is not in creating a disciplined community that can display nonviolence to society. Rather, as seen in King, Tutu, and Chávez, the purpose of Christian nonviolence is to transfigure society into "the beloved community."

---

42. Mennonite theologian Malinda Elizabeth Berry brings these two streams together in what she calls shalom political theology, which draws from Reinhold Niebuhr's realistic theological anthropology and Martin Luther King Jr.'s political nonviolence—along with Mennonite lay theologian and cookbook author Doris Janzen Longacre's nonconformity. See Berry, "Shalom Political Theology," 64–69.

Liberationist Nonviolence

DISRUPTING THE SPIRAL OF VIOLENCE

In 1989, a group of Anabaptist scholars convened to engage one of the most significant theological developments of the twentieth century: Latin American Liberation Theology (LALT).[1] As they assessed LALT, they found many resonances between liberation theology and their own Anabaptist theology. Editor Daniel S. Schipani writes in the introduction to the volume they produced, "We are especially interested in the fact that Latin American Liberation Theology purports to be *a new way of doing theology* that involves far more than a matter of alternative theologizing as an intellectual or academic endeavor. . . . Further, the critique and the alternative perspectives and corrective social action advocated by liberationists in light of the context of oppression within and from which they have reflected, have been reinforced in the last few years by the presence and praxis of the base ecclesial communities as *a new way*

---

1. While this chapter focuses on Latin American Liberation Theology, we acknowledge parallel liberationist movements in Black and feminist theology as well—some of which we discuss in chapters 6 and 8, respectively.

of being the church."[2] In LALT, these Anabaptist theologians had clearly found a kindred spirit.[3] As Schipani writes, the fact that liberationists make "references to a *'new Reformation'* is not surprising."[4]

Schipani and his Anabaptist coauthors identify a number of parallels between LALT and emphases of the sixteenth-century Radical Reformers.[5] However, on at least one point they demur: the question of LALT's allowance for revolutionary violence. In response, liberation theologian José Míguez Bonino states that this is the wrong question with which to begin. He argues that, whether one likes it or not, one is already enmeshed in power structures that involve force and often forms of violence. Thus, for Bonino, "the question is not whether we accept violence or not" but what to do "with the reality of violence in which we are all actively involved."[6]

As we will see in this chapter, one of the unique contributions of liberationist nonviolence is its analysis of violence as a deeper, more pervasive reality than is commonly recognized, even by those otherwise committed to nonviolence. Only when violence is recognized and analyzed in its multifarious forms can nonviolent resistance be offered as a realistic means of overcoming such violence. This means not simply stopping overt acts of bloodshed but also nonviolently confronting systemic injustices at the roots of violence. To demonstrate this approach, we turn to the writings of Latin American Catholic

2. Schipani, introduction to *Freedom and Discipleship*, 2, emphasis original.

3. *Freedom and Discipleship* was published in 1989, one year after Gustavo Gutiérrez's seminal work, *A Theology of Liberation*, had been released in a fifteenth-anniversary edition. It was originally published in Spanish in Lima, Peru, in 1971, and earlier drafts had circulated as early as 1968 when the Medellín Conference (discussed below) took place.

4. Schipani, introduction to *Freedom and Discipleship*, 2, emphasis original.

5. For parallels, see especially Rutschman, "Anabaptism and Liberation Theology."

6. Bonino, "On Discipleship, Justice and Power," 138.

bishops—in particular Archbishops Óscar Romero and Hélder Câmara—before describing how liberationist nonviolence has been put into practice by laity as well through the work of Nobel Laureate Adolfo Pérez Esquivel and other nonviolent Latin American liberationists.

Seeing and Naming Violence

Latin American Liberation Theology arose not primarily out of the theological academy but out of the church. At a 1955 meeting in Rio de Janeiro, Brazil, the Latin American Episcopal Council—better known as CELAM from the Spanish *Consejo Episcopal Latinoamericano*—was formed by Latin American Catholic bishops to address the needs and concerns of their continent.[7] From 1962 to 1965, CELAM pressed the Second Vatican Council to explicitly address the plight of the world's poor, and a Church of the Poor group was established to do just that. The council's *Gaudium et spes*, promulgated by Pope Paul VI at the close of the council on December 7, 1965, identified the Catholic Church's "duty of scrutinizing the signs of the times and of interpreting them in the light of the Gospel."[8] With the encouragement of Pope Paul VI, Latin American bishops took this duty as an invitation to scrutinize the political, social, and economic realities of their Latin American contexts and to interpret them in light of the liberative message of the Gospels.[9]

At the second CELAM conference, convened by Pope Paul VI and held in Medellín, Colombia, in 1968, the bishops effectively launched the movement for Latin American liberation as an explicit contextual application of the Second Vatican

7. See the CELAM website at http://www.celam.org.

8. Paul VI, *Gaudium et spes*, §4.

9. Liberation theologian Leonardo Boff describes how the Second Vatican Council was a point of departure for LALT in Boff, *When Theology Listens to the Poor*, 1–31.

Council. As Venezuelan theologian Rafael Luciani notes, the "conference effected a contextualized reception of Vatican II and thereby gave substance to what had previously been marginal concepts: the church of the poor, and a church committed to the liberation and full flourishing of the needy and the abandoned." Luciani concludes that the Medellín conference "provided the hermeneutical framework for reading the specifically Latin American signs of the times, which was done by applying the see-judge-act method."[10] Unlike nonviolence of Christian discipleship, this method starts not with a deduction from scriptural teachings to pacifism but rather from an inductive process of identifying and scrutinizing the realities on the ground before determining the best way to act to rectify them.

Nearly a decade after the Medellín conference, a group of twenty bishops from nine Latin American countries, along with additional priests and laypeople, met in Bogotá, Colombia, to reflect specifically on "the situation of violence in Latin America—together with the Christian response of nonviolence as a social force and as the liberating answer provided in the gospel itself." The bishops note that "the situation of sin we denounced at our conference in Medellín has continued unabated, if indeed it has not actually deteriorated." As they proceed to identify this situation of sin, they utilize the language of violence. The violence they describe, however, is not a sudden forceful outburst against a backdrop of relative peacefulness. Rather, it is a pervasive backdrop to their societies. "We live in a whole climate of violence," they write.

> There is violence in the area of economics by reason of acute fiscal crises, the repeated devaluation of our currencies, unemployment, and soaring taxes—the burden of which ultimately falls

10. Luciani, "Medellín Fifty Years Later," 567, 589.

on the poor and helpless. There is violence at the political level, as our people in varying degrees are deprived of their right of self-expression and self-determination and of the exercise of their civil rights. Still more grave in many countries are human-rights violations in the form of torture, kidnappings, and murder. Violence also makes its appearance in various forms of delinquency, in drug abuse as an escape from reality, in the mistreatment of women—all tragic expressions of frustration and of the spiritual and cultural decadence of a people losing their hope in tomorrow.[11]

This multifaceted reality of violence is what Óscar Romero confronted when he became archbishop of San Salvador in 1977. Romero did not set out to be a liberation theologian. He distanced himself from the more radical, sociopolitical, Marxist wing of the movement and adhered closely to the Catholic Church's orthodox theology and social teachings.[12] Yet it was precisely because of his adherence to the tradition of Catholic Social Teaching that he became an outspoken voice for the oppressed of El Salvador after he was appointed archbishop. Indeed, Romero saw Catholic Social Teaching as a kind of liberation theology. As Michael Lee observes, if liberation theology is associated with Marxist social analysis, revolutionary violence, and exclusively temporal concerns, then Romero opposes it. However, "if liberation theology is understood broadly as a theology committed to understanding faith as exercised in the pursuit of justice, with principles proclaimed in magisterial teaching . . . , then Romero can be seen as an exemplar."[13]

11. "Declaration of the International Meeting of Latin American Bishops," 118, 119.
12. On the complicated and sometimes ironic relationship between liberation theologians and Catholic orthodoxy, see Carnes, "Reconsideration of Religious Authority," 473–74.
13. Lee, *Revolutionary Saint*, 190–91. For Romero's relation to liberation theology, see also Colón-Emeric, *Óscar Romero's Theological Vision*. For his relation to Catholic Social Teaching, see Whelan, *Blood in the Fields*. Thanks to Matthew Whelan for

In the same vein as the bishops of CELAM, Romero saw violence not as an interruption to the ordinary but as an ordinary facet of the daily lives of Salvadorans. As agricultural land was privatized and concentrated in the hands of wealthy elites, the average Salvadorans lost their means of subsistence. For Romero, this situation is not merely an injustice that leads to violence; it is itself a form of violence. By depriving citizens of land to farm for themselves and their families, the landowners—and the state apparatuses that supported them—were inflicting violence on their fellow Salvadorans.

Matthew Whelan, theologian and Romero interpreter, uses the language of "ordinary violence" to describe the violence Romero identifies and confronts. As Whelan describes, Romero uses a number of vivid images to name such violence. Romero compares "ordinary violence to an invasive weed that has infested a field—a weed like Bermuda grass, whose rhizomes branch downward from nodes beneath the field's surface." Whelan explains how this image "suggests that even when the top growth is removed or dies, the underground shoots survive, with a small piece sufficient for regeneration. The shoots can surface in the same space or move elsewhere to colonize, which leads to Romero's question: 'When the roots are firmly in place, should we be surprised to find new weeds sprouting up everywhere?' Violence continues to proliferate because its rhizomes are already lodged so deeply within the landscape." Likewise, Whelan describes how Romero pictures ordinary violence as "a thick smog filling 'the air we breathe.' We inhale it, he says, in our 'ordinary respiration.' It enters us 'through all the pores of our being.' The violence appears, not as waves on otherwise tranquil waters but as the

_____

clarifying Romero's relationship to liberation theology and drawing our attention to Lee's work.

'tranquil' waters themselves."[14] Thus, for Romero, to see and name violence rightly means identifying the roots and not merely the shoots of violence. It means seeing violence as a pervasive smog or tranquil water and not merely as bullets and bloodshed, though the former often leads to the latter. This ordinary violence, as an assault against human dignity through deprivation of the necessities of life, is then reified in structures and institutions. As Romero writes in his fourth pastoral letter,

> The church condemns "structural" or "institutionalized violence," "the result of an unjust situation in which the majority of men, women, and children in our country find themselves deprived of the necessities of life." The church condemns this violence not only because it is unjust in itself, and the objective expression of personal and collective sin, but also because it is the cause of other innumerable cruelties and more obvious acts of violence.
>
> More and more Salvadorans are learning . . . that the deepest root of the serious evils that afflict us, including the renewed outbreak of violence, is this *structural violence*. It takes concrete form in the unjust distribution of wealth and of property—especially insofar as it includes landownership—and, more generally, in that amalgam of economic and political structures by which the few grow increasingly rich and powerful, while the remainder grow increasingly poor and weak.[15]

For publicly identifying and naming the structural violence of his society, Romero ultimately became its victim. On March 24, 1980, while celebrating the mass at a hospital for the terminally ill, Romero was shot in the heart in an assassination ordered

14. Whelan, "'You Posses the Land That Belongs to All Salvadorans,'" 643, 644.
15. Romero, *Voice of the Voiceless*, 143.

by a right-wing politician described as a "principal henchmen for wealthy landowners."[16]

Overcoming Violence through Strategic Nonviolence

If violence is as pervasive as liberationists describe, then a personal commitment to pacifism will not be sufficient to overcome it.[17] Liberationist nonviolence, then, is not merely about refraining from overt acts of violence; it is about actively working to *undo* the violence that is inimical to human flourishing. As we saw above, some pacifists worry that a recognition of structural or institutional violence will give justification for revolutionary violence in response. But this need not be the case. In his third pastoral letter, for example, Romero condemns revolutionary violence, which he labels "sedition or terrorism," in the strongest terms. He writes, "This form of violence is usually organized and pursued in the form of guerrilla warfare or terrorism and is wrongly thought of as the final and only effective way to change a social situation. It is a violence that produces and

16. Krauss, "U.S., Aware of Killings, Worked with Salvador's Rightists, Papers Suggest." As Krauss describes, investigations traced Romero's assassination to the order of Roberto d'Aubuisson, whom the CIA described as "principal henchman for wealthy landowners and a coordinator of the right-wing death squads that have murdered several thousand suspected leftists and leftist sympathizers during the past year." These findings were covered up by both the Reagan and first Bush administrations, who provided aid to d'Aubuisson in his fight against "leftist guerrillas."

17. Hélder Câmara, discussed below, writes, "I don't like the word 'pacifism.' It sounds too much like 'passivism.' And if it means peace at any price—even at the price of injustice or servitude, for oneself or others—then that of course will never do." He thus addresses pacifists directly:

> I always ask those who in conscience refuse military service, not to sit back and take it easy just because they're officially left alone. My friends, the violence you reject won't disappear or diminish simply because you've chosen not to participate in it! You can't rest on your laurels! You can't wash your hands of violence. If you think violence is an evil, you should also believe that only nonviolence can stop it. You should give nonviolence a push. So give the energy you're not spending in the army to nonviolence and action as a means of resolving conflicts and furthering justice! (Câmara, *Questions for Living*, 88, 89)

provokes useless and unjustifiable bloodshed, abandons society to explosive tensions beyond the control of reason, and disparages in principle any form of dialogue as a possible means of solving social conflicts."[18]

Drawing from Catholic Social Teaching, Romero does believe that there are legitimate forms of violence for self-defense or even, in exceptional cases, for insurrection against prolonged tyranny.[19] As such, while Romero condemns "the cult of violence" and commends "the power of nonviolence," his thinking would best be categorized as a strongly pacifistic interpretation of traditional Catholic just war doctrine rather than as pacifist per se.[20] However, within LALT, there are more outspoken pacifist voices as well. One of them is Archbishop Hélder Câmara.

Dom Hélder Câmara was archbishop of Olinda and Recife, Brazil, from 1964 to 1985. As with Romero, Câmara used his platform to advocate for the poor of his country, even as he was subjected to censorship and threat from Brazil's military dictatorship, which was in power for the duration of his term as archbishop.[21] Unlike Romero, Câmara was an outspoken advocate of liberation theology who took a decidedly nonviolent approach to liberation.[22]

18. Romero, *Voice of the Voiceless*, 107.

19. Romero, *Voice of the Voiceless*, 107, 144–45. Romero is reflecting, in particular, on Paul VI's 1967 *Populorum progressio*, §§30–31.

20. Romero, *Voice of the Voiceless*, 110, 107.

21. For a helpful introduction to Câmara's life and work, see McDonagh, introduction to *Dom Hélder Câmara*. Much of Câmara's writing remains untranslated. For select English-language translations of his writings, see the following Câmara texts: *Church and Colonialism*; *Dom Hélder Câmara*; *Hoping against All Hope*; *Questions for Living*; *Revolution through Peace*; and *Spiral of Violence*. See also the English-language tribute to Câmara's life and work by Schipani and Wessels, *Promise of Hope*.

22. This is not to say that Câmara was necessarily opposed to Catholic Social Teaching. When asked why the church does not denounce the arms race as explicitly as he does, Câmara responded, "The popes, the Council, the bishops' conferences, have done this: there can be no peace without respect for human rights, without justice among nations, without the creation of a world authority able to arbitrate

In a short 1971 tract, *Spiral of Violence*, Câmara succinctly describes the problem he sees in his Latin American context before proposing his answer to it. "It is common knowledge that poverty kills just as surely as the most bloody war. But poverty does more than kill," he writes. "It leads to physical deformity (just think of Biafra), to psychological deformity (there are many cases of mental subnormality for which hunger is responsible), and to moral deformity (those who, through a situation of slavery, hidden but nonetheless real, are living without prospects and without hope, foundering in fatalism and reduced to a begging mentality)." Câmara labels this kind of institutional or structural violence "violence No. 1." As with Romero, Câmara identifies such violence by its pervasiveness, its ordinariness. "You will find that everywhere the injustices are a form of violence," he writes. "One can and must say that they are everywhere the basic violence, violence No. 1."[23]

The natural response to such violence is violent revolt, which Câmara labels "violence No. 2." "Violence attracts violence," he writes. "Let us repeat fearlessly and ceaselessly: injustices bring revolt, either from the oppressed or from the youth, determined to fight for a more just and more human world." Although Câmara writes as someone committed to nonviolence, he does not condemn violence No. 2 in principle. Instead, he argues strategically and pragmatically that revolutionary violence is an ineffective response to institutionalized violence, as it makes "the authorities consider themselves obliged to preserve or re-establish public order, even if this means using force; this is violence No. 3." And so the spiral of violence merely repeats itself, while the legitimate claims for justice on the part

conflicts, and so on. It's not their fault if their proposals get no better reception than their condemnations. Do Christians even know what these proposals are?" Câmara, *Questions for Living*, 81.

23. Câmara, *Spiral of Violence*, 25–26, 29–30.

of the oppressed are ignored for the sake of a false peace, which Câmara likens to "the peace of a swamp with rotten matter fermenting in its depths."[24]

Câmara has no faith in the ability of authoritarian regimes to stop the spiral of violence. Instead, he calls on the oppressed and their allies to break the spiral of violence by taking up a nonviolent alternative to violence No. 2. Drawing on the inspiration of Mohandas Gandhi and Martin Luther King Jr., Câmara calls on his readers to apply "liberating moral pressure" to demand "definite changes in unjust and inhuman structures." Câmara is not naive about the consciences of dictators. He painstakingly details all the ways authoritarian regimes try to stifle even nonviolent protest. But he argues that nonviolent action is the most effective way to engender the sympathies of the people, especially young people, and that change cannot happen without widespread popular support. Those in power will always act in their self-interest, so applying liberating moral pressure to fight injustice is a way to make them see that it is in their own best interest to do what is just. As Câmara writes, "The privileged and the authorities will come to understand that common sense obliges one to choose between bloody and armed violence, on the one hand, and on the other the violence of the peaceful: liberating moral pressure."[25]

Once again, the goal of liberationist nonviolence is not merely to minimize the clash between revolutionary force (violence No. 2) and state force (violence No. 3). Rather, its goal is to address the root cause of such violence: institutional or structural violence (violence No. 1). Nonviolent liberationists are still *liberationists*, so their ultimate goals are "to change the

24. Câmara, *Spiral of Violence*, 34, 55, 33.
25. Câmara, *Spiral of Violence*, 33, 55. Câmara dedicates the pamphlet to the memory of Gandhi and King.

socio-economic, political and cultural structures of the under-developed countries" and "to induce the developed countries to integrate their underdeveloped strata and to revise radically the international policies governing trade with the underdeveloped countries."[26] Câmara elsewhere elaborates: "Generally speaking, the strategy of nonviolent action aims to cause the foundations of unjust power to collapse. Oppressive, repressive power rests on resignation, collaboration, and obedience on the part of the people. Nonviolence tries to organize noncollaboration and disobedience by as many people as possible. No power can last long, even by force of arms, against a whole population that refuses to obey it and recognizes another power instead. The strategy also includes a tireless dialogue with half-hearted agents of unjust power to try to get them to rally to the cause of justice."[27]

In short, the goal is to eliminate violence No. 1 in order to create a more just and equitable world, thereby removing the need for violence No. 2 and breaking the spiral of violence. Câmara thus ends *Spiral of Violence* with a pragmatic call to fellow revolutionaries:

What separates us? We are united in our aims: we wish for a more just and human world. You think perhaps that only armed violence will have the power to shake and demolish the inhuman structures which create slaves.

If I joyfully spend the rest of my life, of my powers, of my energies in demanding justice, but without hatred, without armed violence, through liberating moral pressure, through

26. Câmara, *Spiral of Violence*, 63. In personal correspondence, Daniel Schipani points out that liberation theologies in general are justice oriented but not necessarily peace oriented. One of the distinguishing features of liberationist *nonviolence*, then, is that it aims toward peace-oriented restorative justice rather than retributive justice. For a primer on restorative justice, see Zehr, *Little Book of Restorative Justice*.

27. Câmara, *Questions for Living*, 92.

truth and love, it is because I am convinced that only love is constructive and strong.

I know your sincerity and I respect your choice. Leave no-one indifferent around you. Provoke discussions. Your youth must force people to think and take up a position: let it be uncomfortable, like truth, demanding, like justice.[28]

Liberationist Nonviolence in Action in Latin America

Many laypeople throughout Latin America took up Câmara's challenge. One of them is painter and sculptor Adolfo Pérez Esquivel, who was little known outside of Latin America until he was awarded the Nobel Peace Prize in 1980, much to the surprise of the world community, including Pérez Esquivel himself.[29] In his acceptance speech, Pérez Esquivel dispelled any notion that his work for peace and liberation was that of a solitary individual. "I want to receive this distinction in the name of the people of Latin America," he stated, "and, in a very special way, in the name of the poorest and smallest of my brothers and sisters because they are the most beloved of God. I receive it in the name of my indigenous brothers and sisters, the peasants, workers, and young people—in the name of the thousands of members of religious orders and of men and women of good-will who relinquish their privileges to share the life and path of the poor, and who struggle to build a new society."[30]

While many Nobel Laureates are charismatic, internationally recognized figures who found movements for peace, Pérez Esquivel is an unassuming personality whose Peace and Justice Service (or SERPAJ from the Spanish *Servicio Paz y Justicia*)

28. Câmara, *Spiral of Violence*, 82.
29. Charles Antoine describes the confusion that ensued following the announcement of the unknown Pérez Esquivel as Nobel Peace Prize winner on October 13, 1980. See Antoine, introduction to *Christ in a Poncho*, 1.
30. Pérez Esquivel, *Christ in a Poncho*, 135.

was not about starting a new movement but about organizing movements for peace and justice already taking place across Latin America.[31] As a lay Catholic, Pérez Esquivel was inspired by the example of bishops like Câmara and members of CELAM. He followed the Medellín Conference "with great interest" and credited it with giving the church "motivation to go out to the poor—the motivation for a church that would be more poor, more prophetic, more committed to witness."[32] For his own part, Pérez Esquivel traveled tirelessly throughout Latin America, coordinating the nonviolent work for liberation among the people of various countries. In 1977, when he returned to his native Argentina after a pilgrimage throughout Latin America, the Caribbean, North America, and Europe, he was arrested, jailed for fourteen months during which he was tortured, and then put on house arrest for another fourteen months. On his release, he continued where he left off, traveling throughout Latin America to organize nonviolent movements for peace and justice.[33]

Pérez Esquivel uses the analogy of a battle between the ant and the elephant to describe his work: "True, the elephant is stronger. But the ants . . . well, there are more of us." For Pérez Esquivel, this is crucial for the success of liberationist nonviolence. "Isolation is an obstacle to the effectiveness of nonviolent action," he writes. "So we try to coordinate what is being done almost everywhere."[34] But beyond coordination and training in nonviolent tactics, he allows the work of liberation to arise from communities themselves. In their book *Relentless*

31. See Antoine, introduction to *Christ in a Poncho*, 2. As of the writing of this chapter, Pérez Esquivel is eighty-nine years old and still active. See his writings in Spanish at http://www.adolfoperezesquivel.org.

32. Pérez Esquivel, *Christ in a Poncho*, 16.

33. See Antoine, introduction to *Christ in a Poncho*, 7–8.

34. Pérez Esquivel, *Christ in a Poncho*, 32, 28.

Persistence: Nonviolent Action in Latin America, Philip McManus and Gerald Schlabach compile case histories and testimonies from communities throughout Latin America of liberationist nonviolence in practice.[35] Reflecting on these stories, liberation theologian Leonardo Boff writes, "The theology of liberation is not an alternative to active nonviolence, nor vice versa. On the contrary, they are born of the same inspiration, which is the commitment to transform a violent social reality to one based on justice and fraternity through peaceful means. Theologians of liberation always speak with confidence of the historic power of the poor. The process of liberation comes from the oppressed themselves." "Thus," Boff concludes, "active nonviolence and liberation theology are two facets of a single reality. The two facets are not opposed. On the contrary, they inform and complete each other."[36]

Conclusion

Liberationist nonviolence, perhaps more than any other form of nonviolence we have surveyed, is a particular tradition that arose from a particular people at a particular time and place. As we have seen in this chapter, its genesis can be traced back to the founding of CELAM by Latin American Catholic bishops in 1955 and the response to the Second Vatican Council at the second CELAM conference in Medellín in 1968. It was developed to address the particular social, economic, and political realities of Latin American contexts. And it provides a particular method—the see-judge-act method—to address them.

---

35. Case histories include nonviolent movements in Guatemala, Brazil, Bolivia, Honduras, Uruguay, Chile, Peru, and Nicaragua. For further testimonies of nonviolent action in Latin America, see Pérez Esquivel, *Christ in a Poncho*, 43–116.

36. Boff, foreword to *Relentless Persistence*, ix, x.

At the same time, advocates of liberationist nonviolence con-tend that its method transcends the particularities of time, place, and even religion. Câmara writes that "everywhere there are minorities capable of understanding Action for Justice and Peace and adopting it as a workshop for study and action." He labels such people around the world "Abrahamic minorities"—not because they are identified with Abrahamic religions but "because, like Abraham, we are hoping against all hope." He identifies ecumenical work for liberation being done by Catho-lics and Protestants and reckons that "there must be similar movements within other religions." He therefore declares, "The time has come when each religion must rediscover, in its sacred texts, the truths capable of encouraging the human develop-ment of the outcasts of the modern world and of arousing the consciences of the rich."[37]

As with the political nonviolence of Martin Luther King Jr., then, the question that arises for liberationist nonviolence is what, if anything, makes it specifically Christian. At times, when Câmara describes his own nonviolent convictions, he draws on the language of Christian discipleship. "My personal vocation is that of a pilgrim of peace," he writes. "Personally, I would prefer a thousand times to be killed than to kill." He explains this personal conviction by pointing to the gospel—and in particular to the Beatitudes, which he calls "the quin-tessence of the gospel message."[38] And yet, when he makes his appeal for others to adopt liberationist nonviolence—as opposed to liberationist violence—he appeals not to the gos-pel but to the relative effectiveness of nonviolence in bringing about liberation. After witnessing failed attempts at armed revolt (violence No. 2), which ultimately led not to liberation

---

37. Câmara, *Spiral of Violence*, 69, 71.
38. Câmara, *Church and Colonialism*, 109.

but to counterrevolutionary violence (violence No. 3), Câmara became "more and more certain that liberation could never be achieved through armed struggle."[39] Likewise, Pérez Esquivel points to the ineffectiveness of liberationist violence: "We know too that one evil cannot be cured by another. Evils don't cancel each other out. They total up. . . . We have always questioned armed liberation movements—for fear today's oppressed will become tomorrow's oppressors."[40]

The perennial question for liberationist nonviolence is what happens when it fails to bring about liberation. Romero, as we have seen, leaves the door open for one to "resort to a form of violence, in proportion to the need, only after every other possible peaceful means has been tried."[41] This option seems off the table for Câmara and Pérez Esquivel, who are committed to nonviolence both pragmatically and in principle. But perhaps this dilemma provides an answer to what makes liberationist nonviolence specifically Christian: it requires the faith and hope that, when one chooses to enter the struggle for liberation using the nonviolent means that Jesus himself used, one is acting in accordance with the liberating God made incarnate in Jesus Christ. Liberationist nonviolence thus points toward the significance of martyrdom as the exemplification of what Jesus describes as the love that lays down its life for its friends (John 15:13). The love that works for justice and is prepared to suffer and die for the liberation of others is a cruciform, nonviolent love. This is the love exemplified in the life and death of Saint Óscar Romero.

39. Câmara, *Dom Hélder Câmara*, 83.
40. Pérez Esquivel, *Christ in a Poncho*, 27.
41. Romero, *Voice of the Voiceless*, 145.

Christian Antiviolence

RESISTING SEXUAL AND GENDER-BASED VIOLENCE

In March 2019, Puerto Rican Mennonite educator Elizabeth Soto Albrecht convened fifteen women—theologians, ethicists, educators, and peacemaking practitioners—for a writing consultation at Anabaptist Mennonite Biblical Seminary in Elkhart, Indiana, on the theme Liberating the Politics of Jesus.[1] The combination of this location and theme was not coincidental. These women were meeting in the very building where John Howard Yoder, author of the famous apologetic text for Christian nonviolence, *The Politics of Jesus*, had taught and written for nearly three decades—until a disciplinary process in 1992 led to his dismissal from campus for various acts of sexual violence.[2]

The question of how one of the leading twentieth-century advocates of Christian nonviolence could have engaged in

---

1. For another consultation on violence against women also held at the seminary in 1991, see E. Yoder, *Peace Theology and Violence against Women*. Mennonite pastor and theologian Carol Penner, whose work we discuss below, was present at both consultations.
2. See Goossen, "'Defanging the Beast.'"

violent conduct toward women has vexed many proponents of Christian nonviolence. But to the women gathered for this consultation, the problem with peace theology has always been its failure to see the integral connections between the violence of war and genocide and sexual and gender-based violence. As one of the consultation participants, Hilary Scarsella, observes, "The problem with peace theology in the context of war . . . is not just that it forgets to pay attention to interpersonal violence in addition to state violence, but that it gets war and state violence wrong by not recognizing that each are already sexually violent."[3]

The women at this consultation were not meeting to rehabilitate *The Politics of Jesus* in light of the sexual violence of its author. Instead, they were meeting to liberate the politics of Jesus from *The Politics of Jesus*. In other words, their task was not reviving androcentric peace theology but dismantling it in order to rebuild in its place a theology and ethic of resistance to violence "through the wisdom of women."[4] To do so, they turned not to texts by white, male theologians—except at times by way of critique—but instead to mujerista, womanist, feminist, and queer theologies and to the real-life experiences of women and victim-survivors of sexual violence.[5]

What their collective work developed is a unique approach that is not simply another form of Christian nonviolence but

3. Email correspondence, March 10, 2021.

4. See the subtitle of Albrecht and Stephens, *Liberating the Politics of Jesus: Renewing Peace Theology through the Wisdom of Women.*

5. In this chapter, we follow Traci West's use of the term *victim-survivor* as a rhetorical reminder "of the dual status of women who have been both victimized by violent assault and have survived it." As West observes, "Black women are sometimes denied an opportunity to have their victimization recognized. The strength of their coping and survival abilities is commonly emphasized at the expense of an appreciation of their injury and anguish. Multiple aspects of both victimization and survival are represented in women's experiences of, and reactions to, male violence." *Wounds of the Spirit*, 5.

what we here call *Christian antiviolence*: active resistance to sexual and gender-based forms of violence, whether interpersonal or societal. As we describe in this chapter, Christian antiviolence begins not with abstract theological or ethical principles of nonviolence or even with interpretations of Scripture itself. Rather, it begins with reflection on the experiences of women and sexual minorities—especially victim-survivors of sexual violence—and draws from those experiences to interrogate traditional theological and ethical categories (including traditional peace theologies) and to dismantle the patriarchal and white supremacist systems and structures that perpetuate sexual and gender-based violence.

By exposing the elements internal to Christianity that perpetuate sexual and gender-based violence, proponents of Christian antiviolence offer not only a unique approach to violence but also a unique vision of Christianity itself—one that is liberated from patriarchy, racism, white nationalism, homophobia, and other intrinsically violent ideologies. Recognizing that traditional approaches to Christian nonviolence have been oppressive to women, Christian antiviolence does not insist that women practice nonresistance or even nonviolence in the face of abuse. Instead, Christian antiviolence is about empowering women to resist interpersonal violence and working to undo the societal violence that maintains it. Thus, instead of viewing this stream as simply a subset of Christian nonviolence, it may be better to view it as a movement from nonviolence to violence resistance or antiviolence. In order to trace the contours of Christian antiviolence in this chapter, we draw from the work on sexual and gender-based violence by Elizabeth Albrecht, Traci West, Marie Fortune, and a number of other theologians, ethicists, activists, and advocates.

Centering the Experiences of Women

"Experience, which is the basis for all knowledge, has become the primary source of comprehending sexual violence." So writes pastor, theologian, and victim-survivor advocate Marie Fortune on the opening page of the first chapter of her pioneering 1983 work, *Sexual Violence: The Unmentionable Sin.* According to Fortune, "Sexual violence as a topic for ethical discourse among Christians has gone unaddressed." Fortune considers various explanations for this omission before concluding, "The most significant reason for the silence in ethical discourse is that sexual violence is something which is perceived to happen primarily to women and children and, as such, has not been a priority for most ethicists. The limitations of a patriarchal bias and male experience (which for most male ethicists probably did not include sexual assault) have meant that sexual violence as an experience and as an ethical issue has been overlooked." Fortune writes to ensure that this issue is overlooked no longer. As founding director of the FaithTrust Institute (originally the Center for the Prevention of Sexual and Domestic Violence) in Seattle, Washington, Fortune writes not only out of her own experiences but also out of the stories of sexual violence shared by the victim-survivors with whom she worked.[6]

Following Fortune, one of the defining features of Christian antiviolence is that it begins with and centers on the experiences of victim-survivors. Those working and writing within this stream begin with real-life experiences rather than with a priori theological or theoretical commitments to nonviolence. As Mennonite pastor and peace theologian Carol Penner describes,

6. Fortune, *Sexual Violence: The Unmentionable Sin*, 5, 42, 43. See also Fortune's revised and updated volume, *Sexual Violence: The Sin Revisited*. For information on the FaithTrust Institute, see https://www.faithtrustinstitute.org.

women's experiences are not only a "catalyst" but also an "important source" and "one of the norms" of her constructive feminist peace theology. As she constructs her peace theology, she writes, "A primary criterion for the theology examined and constructed . . . is whether it contributes to or lessens the abuse of women in church and society."[7] This is the criterion by which proponents of Christian antiviolence assess not only Christian theology but also proposals for Christian nonviolence: Do they contribute to or combat sexual and gender-based violence?

In her 1999 book, *Wounds of the Spirit: Black Women, Violence, and Resistance Ethics,* Traci West centers the experiences of Black women in her development of an ethic of resistance to interpersonal violence. She writes, "It is by personally listening to women that I have come to recognize the specific, interwoven nature of the intimate and systemic violence African-American women face." West describes her process as follows: "Methodologically, I maintain the concrete suffering of black women victim-survivors as my criterion for evaluating the moral harm generated by intimate violence. I focus specifically on the ways in which women are compelled to assume the qualities of shamefulness and invisibility, and examine how these socially induced responses further contribute to their emotional and spiritual trauma in the aftermath of male assault. Then, by unearthing the ideologies that devalue and dismiss their personhood, I reveal further dimensions of the social constructions that compound the debilitating consequences of intimate violence." West's work thus moves through the stages of carefully listening to women's stories and hearing their anguish before

---

7. C. Penner, "Mennonite Silences and Feminist Voices," 1, 13–14. For other works on interpersonal and sexual violence that center the experiences of victim-survivors, see Albrecht, *Family Violence*; Heggen, *Sexual Abuse*; Krall, *Elephant in God's Living Room*; Scarsella and Krehbiel, "Sexual Violence." See also Smith, *Touched*, for a first-person account by a survivor and New Testament scholar.

assessing the causes of their suffering and developing methods of resistance. Doing so ensures that her proposals for resisting and overcoming violence against women are not simply theoretical but include "tangible, ethical" practices of communal resistance, some of which we discuss below.[8]

Violence as Violation

Based on the experiences of victim-survivors, those writing on interpersonal violence define violence as encompassing more than bloodshed or acts of direct forceful aggression. Just as liberationist nonviolence expands the definition of violence to include economic oppression, so too Christian antiviolence expands the definition to include any violation of bodily or psychological integrity. Fortune describes sexual violence as, "first and foremost, an act of violence, hatred, and aggression." It is like other acts of violence in that "there is a violation of and injury to victims," whether those injuries be "psychological or physical" (or, more often, both). For Fortune, sexual violence is primarily about violence and only secondarily about the sexual nature of that violence. What makes it violence, for Fortune, is not that it is sexual but that it is "a profound violation of another person which is injurious and destructive." She describes rape and child abuse less as "sexual in nature" and more as "acts of violence which are injurious." Thus, for Fortune, "the sexual nature of sexual violence is irrelevant. Violence is violence no matter what form it takes. The body is assaulted, injury occurs, and there is the experience of physical

---

8. West, *Wounds of the Spirit*, vii, 1, 2, 193. Leah Thomas observes that West's approach is intentionally multidisciplinary, drawing not only from Christian theology and ethics but also from theories of violence that have been historically neglected within Christian thought (email correspondence, February 21, 2021). For Thomas's own proposal for anti-racist pastoral care inspired by West's multidisciplinary approach, see L. Thomas, *Just Care*.

and emotional pain." At the same time, sexual violence is in many ways *especially* violent. "Any victim of rape knows that she has experienced the most violent act possible short of murder," Fortune writes. "And any victim of child sexual abuse is haunted by the helplessness she felt at the hands of the molester who sought to control and exploit her. . . . The nature of the assault makes clear the totality of the violation of the person. During the attack or abuse, the victim is not only out of control of her/his situation, but the victim is also assaulted in the most vulnerable dimension of the self."[9]

As Elizabeth Albrecht describes, in addition to overt acts of interpersonal violence, sexual violence also "includes hidden or covert violence that does not necessarily do direct physical harm but nonetheless destroys human dignity." She cites mental health clinician and pastoral theologian Ruth Krall, who describes such violence as "a violation of personhood." Albrecht explains, "It is the subtle, institutionalized destruction of human possibilities that is around us all the time, although it may not be apparent to those who are comfortably situated. It is present, nonetheless, whenever the structures of society act to depersonalize human beings, and we need to be aware that our social and political systems can actually embed violence."[10]

For Hilary Scarsella and Stephanie Krehbiel, directors of the survivor-led and survivor-supporting organization Into Account,[11] sexual violence is "any mode of interpersonal or systemic abuse, coercion, manipulation, silencing, or violence that has a sexual form or expression, a sexual logic, or

9. Fortune, *Sexual Violence: The Unmentionable Sin*, 5–7.

10. Albrecht, *Family Violence*, 17, citing an email exchange with Ruth Krall.

11. Krehbiel is executive director, and Scarsella is director of theological integrity. They are joined in their work by Jay Yoder, director of operations and cofounder. See https://intoaccount.org.

both." They therefore identify sexual violence as "always, simultaneously, both interpersonal and systemic." This interconnectedness between the interpersonal and systemic dimensions of sexual violence means that in order to fully comprehend and combat sexual violence one must "become able to critically analyze multiple and intersecting dynamics of social power as they relate to sexual violence." These dynamics include gender, race, colonialism, political struggle, war, genocide, heterosexism, ableism, and, significantly, Christian theology itself.[12]

Interrogating Christian Theology and Ethics

"We must measure Christian ethics," writes West, "by the extent to which its rhetoric on violence is applicable to the circumstances of women's lives. This is the proper test of the viability and adequacy of its moral prescriptions."[13] Measured by this test, much Christian theology and ethics has been found wanting. As Fortune writes, "Christian ethics and theology have provided little guidance in understanding the difference between sexual activity and sexual violence for a society faced daily with experiences that reflect the confusion between the two. Christian sexual ethics have often promoted the confusion of sexual activity with sexual violence. Furthermore, Christian ethics have failed to confront the problem of sexual violence

12. Scarsella and Krehbiel, "Sexual Violence." As with some of the other figures discussed in this chapter, Scarsella and Krehbiel are writing not out of the framework of peace theology or nonviolence but rather from the frameworks of intersectional, queer, and feminist theologies. Indeed, as we will see below, in many ways their work is committed to dismantling Christian peace theology as traditionally understood. Nevertheless, in doing so their work highlights how resistance to violence can be found in various streams of theological discourse and is not the exclusive right of the Historic Peace Churches and their theologians.

13. West, *Wounds of the Spirit*, 185.

itself; thus, there has been no mandate for Christians to address this widespread problem."[14]

Christian theology and ethics have failed not only by confusion and omission; in many ways, Christian theology and ethics are *intertwined* with sexual violence. As Scarsella and Krehbiel describe, "Sexual violence is not a phenomenon that can be neatly separated from Christian theology," nor is it "a self-contained social malady that merely infiltrates and aggrieves Christian communities in the manner of an outside intruder." Rather, certain tenets of Christian teaching are "linked with the perpetuation of sexual and gendered forms of abuse." This means that, in order to practice resistance to interpersonal violence, Christians must be willing to interrogate Christian teaching itself so they can identify where and how it perpetuates violence and how to extricate Christian teaching from these violent elements. Here we discuss the Christian teachings Scarsella and Krehbiel identify as particularly harmful to women and victim-survivors: atonement, sin, forgiveness, and obedience.[15]

One central tenet of a historically dominant stream of Christian teaching is that Jesus's suffering and death were necessary for the redemption of humanity. A corollary to this teaching is that Christians—who look to Jesus as the model for humanity—should follow Jesus in accepting redemptive suffering as well. As we have seen in previous chapters, this latter teaching is especially prevalent in forms of Christian nonviolence that emphasize discipleship to Jesus or a mystical connection between Christians and the suffering Christ. However, as Mennonite psychotherapist Carolyn Holderread Heggen observes, "In an atmosphere which glorifies suffering, females tend to see

---

14. Fortune, *Sexual Violence: The Unmentionable Sin*, 5–7.
15. Scarsella and Krehbiel, "Sexual Violence."

abuse as their cross to bear, as their way of identifying with the sufferings of Christ. This may result in a pattern of endurance which minimizes the offensiveness of abuse and fosters the acceptance of victimization."[16]

Carol Penner describes the effect this teaching has on victim-survivors: "An abused woman who encountered this theology would find no hope. If she were to avoid the cross of her suffering, she would be told that she is denying the possibility of resurrection. The only liberation offered is heavenly and it can only be gained through death. A woman who resisted a sexual assault would wonder whether she had acted in an un-Christian way by not submitting to the assault and accepting possible death." After analyzing the writings on suffering by John Howard Yoder in particular, Penner concludes, "It would seem that the writings of Yoder have a specific message which women who are being abused can read. This message is that suffering is the badge of the true Christian."[17]

Scarsella and Krehbiel describe two features of traditional atonement doctrine as especially problematic: its "valorization of victimhood" and its rejection of victim-survivors' "assertion of autonomy over their bodies." They conclude, "When willing, violent, abusive self-sacrifice is held to be the source of salvation and, therefore, the quintessential expression of Christian piety, the self-preserving steps necessary for resisting sexual violence become heretical by relation."[18]

Another tenet of traditional Christian theology is that sinfulness—sometimes described in terms of original sin or even total depravity—is a universal human condition. Yet oftentimes this teaching is applied in the church in gendered and racialized

16. Heggen, *Sexual Abuse*, 94.
17. C. Penner, "Mennonite Silences and Feminist Voices," 30, 48.
18. Scarsella and Krehbiel, "Sexual Violence."

ways. Heggen describes how the fall is often blamed in particular on Eve, the woman, thus perpetuating the notion that women are especially morally defective and vulnerable to deception. Not only does such teaching have a negative effect on women's self-esteem and emotional and psychological well-being; according to Heggen, it can also make women more vulnerable to abuse and manipulation. "A female who believes she is morally wrong in a given situation will find it hard to confront an abusive man, particularly if he tells her, 'It's all in your head,' or 'You're just imagining things,'" writes Heggen. "When females can't trust themselves, they easily give up their power and ability to resist things done to them, particularly by a male."[19]

West describes the racial dimensions of these stereotypes of female moral and intellectual inferiority. When women are viewed as liars, emotionally unstable, or inherently unreliable, they are less likely to be believed when they report instances of sexual violence. West describes how one Black woman's repeated reports of abuse were discounted by police "partly because she was dark-skinned and did not show bruises as readily." Moreover, when Black women report abuse by Black men, writes West, "their statements, deemed lies, even about verbal male sexual intimidation, may be construed as tantamount to causing the murder of black men. In this way, both the legitimacy of a woman's racial identity and her truthfulness are impugned. She is assigned the role of victimizer, and implicated in the commission of heinous brutality." In other words, due to systemic oppression of Black people in a culture dominated by whiteness, Black culture has developed a protective dynamic around Black men, which can pressure Black women to remain silent about abuse they suffer at the hands of Black men.[20]

19. Heggen, *Sexual Abuse*, 89.
20. West, *Wounds of the Spirit*, 123, 126.

Further still, cultural stereotypes of Black women as inherently lazy, promiscuous, irresponsible, or reliant on government assistance "can exert pressure on women who are in situations of domestic violence" to stay in those abusive relationships in order to avoid validating these demeaning stereotypes. West summarizes, "The assertion of shameful sexual proclivities as an intrinsic character defect, along with other distorting claims about black women's roles in the family and community, develop a cumulative avalanche of ideology. They inform the contemporary identity of black women, depicting them as women who 'naturally' need to be reformed and controlled. Regulatory, even punitive, public responses to black women seem appropriate and all too reasonable. Male violence against them is given yet another 'rational' basis. Communal numbness to the terrorizing effects of that violence evolves further. Meanwhile, women become well-rehearsed in the practice of self-blame."[21]

While the doctrine of sin can perpetuate sexual violence by demeaning women, the Christian teaching of forgiveness can perpetuate sexual violence by pressuring women to quickly forgive those who have harmed or are still actively harming them. As Scarsella and Krehbiel describe, the Christian teaching of forgiveness is a double-edged sword for victim-survivors. "While direct perpetrators of sexual violence often use the concept of forgiveness to secure a victim's silence," they write, "it is also common that Christian faith leaders and communities will pressure a victim to forgive their perpetrator. In either case, the concept of forgiveness is wielded as both a silencing tool and a mechanism for enabling abuse to continue."[22]

In addition to facing pressure from abusers, faith leaders, and religious communities to offer forgiveness, victim-survivors

21. West, *Wounds of the Spirit*, 134, 137.
22. Scarsella and Krehbiel, "Sexual Violence."

also often face internal pressure to forgive based on the conception of God taught to them by these faith leaders and communities. West observes, "Christian teachings that emphasize 'turning the other cheek' as a paramount virtue for believers may also influence women to view God's love and support as conditional upon their forgiveness of the perpetrator. Family, friends, and clergy often advise women that to 'forgive and forget' is the only appropriate 'Christian response.' She must forgive the abuser to be worthy of God's redeeming love, and to receive full acceptance among the faithful of the church." West describes how the Christian doctrines of sin and forgiveness can have a leveling effect by conveying that all humans are equally sinful and in need of forgiveness. The effect is that "the dividing lines between victim and violent perpetrator can be blurred or erased under this doctrine." Not only are victim-survivors pressured to forgive their abusers; they also become weighed down by shame over the very offenses committed against them. West describes how "the multiedged shame that is generated in black women victim-survivors of intimate violence is a powerful covert weapon of domination" that "functions as an efficient tool of subjugation that teaches women to recognize their own lack of worth." For West, this demoralizing process is itself a form of male violence that "constitutes a moral assault."[23]

Finally, Scarsella and Krehbiel describe how Christian teaching on obedience can be used to manipulate victim-survivors into submission to their male abusers, who are placed in a position over them that is analogous to the patriarchal conception of a God who "requires dutiful obedience above all else."[24] As West describes, "This problem may be

23. West, *Wounds of the Spirit*, 75, 76.
24. Scarsella and Krehbiel, "Sexual Violence."

heightened when a woman's spirituality is shaped in terms of a theological belief in a judgmental male God who calls her to an unattainable state of 'perfect obedience' to 'Him.' The destructive emotional tether that binds a woman to the abuser in her life may be both validated and replicated in her way of imaging and relating to the Divine. God, like her abuser, is punitive and distant. In this way, patriarchal Christian imagery can solidify the emotional bondage of the victim-survivor."[25]

Carol Penner describes how the teaching of obedience has been especially significant for peace theology that emphasizes obedience to God, despite the consequences. Referring to John Howard Yoder's theology specifically, she writes, "The message which Yoder's theology conveys to a woman experiencing abuse is that she should be obedient to her husband. She is encouraged to see herself following in the footsteps of Jesus, who was also obedient."[26] Thus, as Kimberly L. Penner observes, "a theology of obedience is not safe for those with less power in a relationship of unequal power and privilege."[27]

Dismantling Patriarchy and White Supremacy

Having identified various ways Christian theology and ethics can and do perpetuate sexual violence, one might consider Christianity and antiviolence as mutually exclusive. While some committed to antiviolence have come to this conclusion and left Christianity behind, others have sought to recover elements within Christianity that aid in the process of confronting and dismantling patriarchy and white supremacy within the church and wider society. Sometimes this involves rereading Scripture

25. West, *Wounds of the Spirit*, 61.
26. C. Penner, "Mennonite Silences and Feminist Voices," 46.
27. K. Penner, "Mennonite Peace Theology and Violence against Women," 290.

through the lens of victim-survivors in order to recover suppressed perspectives within the texts themselves; other times it involves reformulating Christian doctrines so that instead of supporting patriarchy and white supremacy, they become the very tools for dismantling them.[28]

West calls Christian communities to come alongside women who "initiate resistance on behalf of themselves and in so doing advance the interests of a civil society," enlisting Christian ethics in this project of constructing what she calls an "ethic of violence resistance." Such a Christian social ethic begins with an unflinching "commitment to taking violence against African-American women seriously." Doing so exposes the ways white supremacy, patriarchy, and sexual and gender-based violence are intimately connected. An ethic of violence resistance therefore must involve not only empowering women to resist abusive partners but also committing the church to dismantle white supremacy and patriarchy within it and its surrounding society.[29]

West calls for a number of tangible communal practices of resistance, such as creating performance art that enables participants to rehearse and imagine forms of resistance, encouraging "unruly behavior in girls and women that fuels a defiant spirit in them," providing women-empowering anti-violence training, building women-empowering networks, and insisting on justice-making processes and accountability in response to violence rather than insisting on quick forgiveness. Fully aware of the ways Christian theology has enabled white supremacy and patriarchy, West nevertheless draws from the resources of Christian theology for these practices of resistance:

28. See, for example, Albrecht and Stephens, *Liberating the Politics of Jesus*, especially part 1, "Retrieval, Remembering, and Re-envisioning," and part 3, "Salvation, Redemption, and Witness"; and Larry, *Leaving Silence*.

29. West, *Wounds of the Spirit*, 181–82.

The requisite Christian engagement in definite practices that uphold women's genuine moral worth can be called "truth-work." Truth-work exemplifies an important tenet of the Christian faith that commends the appropriation of Jesus Christ as truth. This appropriation does not consist of an intellectual assent, rather it demands a specific praxis. Knowing and doing are thoroughly interlocked in this christological understanding. In the Christian faith, to know Jesus is to participate in the ways of Jesus. This kind of "knowing and doing" involves an interactive process of becoming empowered. It involves reaching outside oneself to stretch and grow toward the embodiment of justice, and reaching within oneself to tap rich inner resources of courage and passion. To recognize what is truly just, Christians rely upon their ability to access power from God, their communities of accountability, and resources within themselves. They can live out this realization of truth by working to create conditions in the world that reflect it. This process of participating in the incarnation of justice requires literal engagement with distorting human realities such as violence, white supremacy, and male dominance. It means doing the work that enables the truth of human wholeness, worth, and dignity to be fulfilled.[30]

Having enlisted the church and Christian ethics and theology in the process of dismantling patriarchy and white supremacy, West concludes with a number of practical "resistance strategies" for the church, beginning with "continual self-critique that focuses on eliminating acts of violence among its members and ferreting out messages that reinforce the acceptability of violence against women within its traditions and practices." Such self-critique can come in the form of a regular audit of liturgies, practices, theological teachings, and orga-

30. West, *Wounds of the Spirit*, 193–99, quotes from 194, 198–99.

nizational structures that subjugate women as well as directly confronting any violence and abuse taking place within the church.[31]

West argues that, in addition to extirpating patriarchy, white supremacy, and violence from within, churches can develop rituals, training, and resources for members to learn to resist these oppressive forces within society. Churches also have a role in teaching congregants a communal ethic that emphasizes both "corporate sinfulness" and "how a communal Christian response can be a sustaining resource in the midst of individual struggles for wholeness that church members face." Finally, West sees a role for churches in documenting "women's stories of abuse and resistance." Churches can monitor "the public and private neighborhood and community agencies that immediately respond to the crisis of violence against women" and advocate for women and victim-survivors at both local and national levels—including advocating "for connections between violence against women, white supremacy, and patriarchy to be spelled out and incorporated into the law school education and law enforcement training of prosecutors, judges, and police personnel." Churches can also play a key role in initiating community conversations and consultations on "specific racial and gender issues that reinforce violence against black women." In all these ways, the church can begin to dismantle patriarchy and white supremacy from within and thereby move from being an oppressive institution in women's lives to being a liberating one.[32]

31. West, *Wounds of the Spirit*, 199–200. See also Brown and Bohn, *Christianity, Patriarchy, and Abuse*; Fortune, *Is Nothing Sacred?*; Heggen, *Sexual Abuse*; Krall, *Elephant in God's Living Room*; Krehbiel, "Pacifist Battlegrounds"; Rutter, *Sex in the Forbidden Zone*.

32. West, *Wounds of the Spirit*, 200–206, quotes from 203, 204, 205, 206.

Conclusion

In this chapter, we have described Christian antiviolence as focused largely on resisting sexual and gender-based violence and the structures that enable it, especially within the church. But as we said at the outset, it would be a mistake to draw a sharp distinction between sexual and gender-based violence and the violence of war and genocide. The reality is that, as women are empowered in the church and society, they are leading the way in resisting not only sexual and gender-based violence but also the violence of war and genocide, which virtually always includes sexual and gender-based violence in addition to the violence of combat.

The reality of women's leadership in resisting the violence of war and genocide is sometimes obscured by the way war stories are told. As Liberian peace activist and 2011 Nobel Laureate Leymah Gbowee observes, "In the traditional telling of war stories, women are always in the background. Our suffering is just a sidebar to the main tale; when we're included, it's for 'human interest.' If we are African, we are even more likely to be marginalized and painted as pathetic—hopeless expressions, torn clothes, sagging breasts. Victims. That is the image of us that the world is used to, and the image that sells."[33]

Through stories like Gbowee's own of organizing the Women of Liberia Mass Action for Peace that was largely responsible for ending the Second Liberian Civil War in 2003, that narrative is starting to change. Gbowee began her career in trauma healing, where she became aware of her own trauma from the abuse she had suffered at the hands of an intimate partner. Out of this work and these experiences—as well as her study of peace theologians and activists—Gbowee

33. Gbowee, *Mighty Be Our Powers*, vii.

organized a grassroots movement for peace among Liberian women, which drew international attention for its tactics, including a sex strike to end the war. This movement ultimately led not only to the end of the civil war but also to the election of the first woman president of any country in Africa, when fellow nonviolent activist Ellen Johnson Sirleaf was elected president of Liberia in 2005.[34] Gbowee's story and many others like hers around the world demonstrate how resistance to interpersonal violence and resistance to war ultimately go hand in hand.[35]

34. Sirleaf and Gbowee received the Nobel Peace Prize together, along with Tawak-kol Karman of Yemen. For more details on this movement, see Gbowee, *Mighty Be Our Powers*, and the 2008 documentary *Pray the Devil Back to Hell*, directed by Gini Reticker and narrated by Gbowee.

35. For other examples of women-led movements for peace, see West, *Solidarity and Defiant Spirituality*; Cahill, *Blessed Are the Peacemakers*, 333–38; and Lozano, "Women of Faith Advocating Peace in Colombia."

Conclusion

In this book, we have discussed eight broad streams of Christian nonviolence or antiviolence and interacted with numerous thinkers and activists who represent each. It would be tempting by way of conclusion to offer a grand, Hegelian synthesis of these streams as one unified raging river of Christian nonviolence. Doing so, however, would fail to do justice to the particularities of each stream, especially those points where they have legitimate differences from one another.

Another temptation would be to line each stream up in terms of the dichotomy Reinhold Niebuhr and others (including many pacifists) have imposed on Christian nonviolence: faithful versus effective, communal versus political, quietist versus activist, absolutist versus flexible, and so on. While the structure of this book offered a nod to Niebuhr's distinction—with the first four chapters representing streams typically thought to be more in the "faithfulness" camp and the last four representing streams typically thought to be more in the "effectiveness" camp—our discussion of these streams has shown that, by and large, these dichotomies fail to hold up once the nuances of each stream are seen and appreciated. These dualistic categories therefore tend to generate more heat than light when it comes to understanding the deeper moral logic of the respective streams.

As we mentioned in the introduction, we see Christian nonviolence not as a settled position, pair of positions, or even variety of positions; rather, we see it as a form (or forms) of Spirit-led moral discernment about that which is "good and acceptable and perfect" in God's world (Rom. 12:2). The eight streams we have described, then, reach the conclusions they do because of different underlying theo-logics that animate them. A more fruitful way to understand each of these streams and how they relate to and differ from one another, then, is to ask how they intersect with other theological or ethical loci: God, Scripture, humanity, sin, redemption, church, eschatology, and so on. Throughout the chapters, we have touched on these themes when they arise from the figures we discuss rather than running each stream through a grid of systematic theology. Nevertheless, when we view the streams through the lenses of these various loci, we can see them merging and diverging in interesting and unexpected ways.

One theological locus does deserve sustained attention in relation to Christian nonviolence, and that is the doctrine of creation. As we have described through the various figures discussed in this book, Christian nonviolence addresses violence that attends not only to international conflicts but also to national forms of injustice, church divisions, and interpersonal conflicts. Each stream, in one form or another, is concerned with bringing the peace of God to a broken world, and each enters into complex forms of conflict in order to do so. But most of the forms of conflict we have described have edges and limits. A war may draw in actors from beyond a particular region, for example, but only rarely are wars truly global. In contrast, creation care in an age of climate change poses a new, truly global set of challenges for those committed to Christian nonviolence of any form to take up in earnest—in particular, the slow violence that imposes itself first on the most vulnerable and ultimately on the entire world.[1]

Discussions of Christian obligations to nonhuman creation provide a helpful entry point, extending our thinking about the value of life to the rest of creation with which humans are interwoven.[2] But even if thinking is restricted to how humans harm other humans through contributions to a changing climate, there are new challenges that climate change poses, as a diffuse form of harm done by humans against one another. For with human contributions to climate change, it is frequently difficult to attribute responsibility for the harm done: a large factory may introduce more pollutants into the atmosphere than an individual household, but both contribute to an overall condition that all must inherit.

In line with the approach to Christian nonviolence presented here, Mark Douglas has recently argued that traditions of Christian nonviolence are best understood not as a pristine position from which Christian history has fallen but as practical wisdom that can be flexibly appropriated to face new challenges.[3] Using the lessons learned from past practitioners, Christians can apply those same lessons to new and novel forms of violence without fearing that some purity of practice is being lost.[4] For as we have seen, Christian nonviolence encompasses questions that are both material and immaterial, addressing both virtuous living and just distribution of goods, making space for the need

1. See Nixon, *Slow Violence and the Environmentalism of the Poor*.
2. Wennberg, *God, Humans and Animals*, 119–48, details some of the issues with assuming that moral obligations extend only to those we have social contracts with or only to those with whom humans can communicate. See also York and Alexis-Baker, *Faith Embracing All Creatures*.
3. Douglas, *Christian Pacifism for an Environmental Age*, 77–81.
4. Douglas, *Christian Pacifism for an Environmental Age*, 103.

both to tend to wounds and to oppose those parts of human existence that cause the wounds. Christian nonviolence, in other words, has expanded its repertoire and offered new gifts to bind new wounds, without ceasing to be Christian.

For Christian nonviolence to live into the future, it not only must address itself to the old ways of violence, such as those discussed throughout this book, but also must include a vision for addressing the corruption of a shared creation. Perhaps most intuitively, there is a way for political nonviolence to apply itself not just to social violence and war but also to climate change.[5] But this is certainly not the fullness of what is needed or the end of what Christian nonviolence has to offer to a global problem like climate change. From liberationist nonviolence, we learn to see that Indigenous peoples and the most vulnerable should take center stage in our constructive proposals about how our shared world should be ordered.[6] From realist nonviolence, we learn that Christians must think practically and sober-mindedly about reducing consumption and identifying and reining in bad actors. From apocalyptic nonviolence, we see that nonviolence is not simply about refraining from doing harm but also about opposing those entities that do harm environmentally—those entities still under the sway of the power of Death writ large. The various ways of engaging climate change as a public form of violence are enriched and deepened by learning from the various streams of this book in their own light.

But nonviolent engagement with climate change also means learning the lessons that go beyond public advocacy. From the

5. Kevin O'Brien views nonviolence as offering primarily a political response, reading both Dorothy Day and César Chávez through this lens. As we have shown in this book, political nonviolence is one way to appropriate these thinkers, but O'Brien's reading assumes this is the primary mode by which Christian nonviolence contributes to this question. See K. O'Brien, *Violence of Climate Change*.

6. See, for example, Augustine, *Land Is Not Empty*.

stream of nonviolence as Christian virtue, we learn that Christians must distinguish between what they need and what they want and must love Earth's resources well without becoming greedy for more than is needed. From nonviolence of Christian discipleship, we learn how Christians might pilot and model new forms of consumption, of land arrangements, and of giving and sacrifice for one's neighbor that can be a witness to the wider world. From nonviolence of Christian mysticism, we learn how Christians can come to view their own lives as interconnected with creation and with their distant neighbors. From Christian antiviolence, we learn how to see the gendered ways in which the slow violence of climate change occurs and how women, sexual minorities, and victim-survivors can lead the way to true *shalom*, or well-being, which is not only the absence of violence but also the presence of justice and flourishing for all.

As we move further into the twenty-first century, we can continue to learn from the great cloud of witnesses to Christian nonviolence in its many forms from the twentieth and early twenty-first centuries that we have surveyed in this book. What is ultimately needed to face new challenges will not be a single, unified form of Christian nonviolence but a proliferation of new forms, each drawing wisdom from the past while looking ahead to ever-evolving challenges. This will mean the willingness of proponents of each stream to acknowledge that those from the other streams are likewise anticipating the peace of God in their practice and witness and to creatively and patiently live in witness to the Prince of Peace, who heals the world of all the various forms of violence in it.

BIBLIOGRAPHY

Albrecht, Elizabeth Soto. *Family Violence: Reclaiming a Theology of Nonviolence.* Maryknoll, NY: Orbis Books, 2008.

Albrecht, Elizabeth Soto, and Darryl W. Stephens, eds. *Liberating the Politics of Jesus: Renewing Peace Theology through the Wisdom of Women.* New York: T&T Clark, 2020.

Alexis-Baker, Andy. "Community, Policing, and Violence." *Conrad Grebel Review* 26, no. 2 (2008): 102–16.

———. "The Gospel or a Glock? Mennonites and the Police." *Conrad Grebel Review* 25, no. 2 (2007): 23–49.

Allison, James. *Raising Abel: The Recovery of the Eschatological Imagination.* New York: Herder and Herder, 1996.

Antoine, Charles. Introduction to *Christ in a Poncho*, by Pérez Esquivel, 1–12.

Augustine. *Letter 189* (to Boniface). In *War and Christian Ethics*, 2nd ed., edited by Arthur F. Holmes, 61–63. Grand Rapids: Baker Academic, 2005.

Augustine, Sarah. *The Land Is Not Empty: Following Jesus in Dismantling the Doctrine of Discovery.* Harrisonburg, VA: Herald, 2021.

Azaransky, Sarah. *This Worldwide Struggle: Religion and the International Roots of the Civil Rights Movement.* Oxford: Oxford University Press, 2017.

Baldwin, Lewis V. "Rufus Burrow, Jr., Personal Idealism, and the Life and Thought of Martin Luther King, Jr." *Pluralist* 6 (2011): 1–13.

Battle, Michael. *Reconciliation: The Ubuntu Theology of Desmond Tutu.* Cleveland: Pilgrim, 1997.

Beckley, Harlan. *Passion for Justice: Retrieving the Legacies of Walter Rauschenbusch, John A. Ryan, and Reinhold Niebuhr*. Louisville: Westminster John Knox, 1992.

Bell, Daniel M., Jr. *Just War as Christian Discipleship: Recentering the Tradition in the Church Rather than the State*. Grand Rapids: Baker Academic, 2009.

Benedict XVI. "Fighting Poverty to Build Peace." Vatican Library. January 1, 2009. https://www.vatican.va/content/benedict-xvi/en/messages/peace/documents/hf_ben-xvi_mes_20081208_xlii-world-day-peace.html.

———. "If You Want to Cultivate Peace, Protect Creation." Vatican Library. January 1, 2010. https://www.vatican.va/content/benedict-xvi/en/messages/peace/documents/hf_ben-xvi_mes_20091208_xliii-world-day-peace.html.

Bennett, Thomas Andrew. *Labor of God: The Agony of the Cross as the Birth of the Church*. Waco: Baylor University Press, 2017.

Berrigan, Daniel. *Exodus: Let My People Go*. Eugene, OR: Cascade Books, 2015.

———. *The Geography of Faith: Conversations between Daniel Berrigan, When Underground, and Robert Coles*. Boston: Beacon, 1972.

———. *No Gods but One*. Grand Rapids: Eerdmans, 2009.

Berry, Malinda Elizabeth. "Shalom Political Theology: A New Type of Mennonite Peace Theology for a New Era of Discipleship." *Conrad Grebel Review* 34, no. 1 (2016): 49–73.

Biggar, Nigel. *In Defence of War*. Oxford: Oxford University Press, 2013.

Boff, Leonardo. Foreword to *Relentless Persistence*, by McManus and Schlabach, vii–xi.

———. *Virtues for Another Possible World*. Eugene, OR: Cascade Books, 2011.

———. *When Theology Listens to the Poor*. Translated by Robert R. Barr. San Francisco: Harper & Row, 1988.

Bonhoeffer, Dietrich. *Discipleship*. Dietrich Bonhoeffer Works 4. Minneapolis: Fortress, 2003.

———. *Ethics*. Dietrich Bonhoeffer Works 6. Minneapolis: Fortress, 2005.

———. *Life Together*. Dietrich Bonhoeffer Works 5. Minneapolis: Fortress, 2005.

Bonino, José Míguez. "On Discipleship, Justice and Power." In Schipani, *Freedom and Discipleship*, 131–38.

Brimlow, Robert W. *What about Hitler? Wrestling with Jesus's Call to Non-violence in an Evil World*. Grand Rapids: Brazos, 2006.

Brock, Peter. *Pacifism in Europe to 1914*. Princeton, NJ: Princeton University Press, 1972.

———. *Pacifism in the United States: From the Colonial Era to the First World War*. Princeton, NJ: Princeton University Press, 2015.

Brown, Joanne Carlson, and Carole R. Bohn, eds. *Christianity, Patriarchy, and Abuse: A Feminist Critique*. New York: Pilgrim, 1989.

Burkholder, J. Lawrence. "Concluding Postscript." In *The Limits of Perfection: A Conversation with J. Lawrence Burkholder*, 2nd ed., edited by Rodney J. Sawatsky and Scott Holland, 143–48. Kitchener, ON: Pandora, 1993.

———. "How Do We Do Peace Theology?" In *Essays on Peace Theology and Witness*, edited by Willard M. Swartley, 12–34. Elkhart, IN: Institute of Mennonite Studies, 1988.

———. "The Limits of Perfection: Autobiographical Reflections." In *The Limits of Perfection: A Conversation with J. Lawrence Burkholder*, 2nd ed., edited by Rodney J. Sawatsky and Scott Holland, 1–54. Kitchener, ON: Pandora, 1993.

———. *Mennonite Ethics: From Isolation to Engagement*. Edited by Lauren Friesen. Victoria, BC: Friesen, 2018.

———. *The Problem of Social Responsibility from the Perspective of the Mennonite Church*. Elkhart, IN: Institute of Mennonite Studies, 1989.

———. *Recollections of a Sectarian Realist: A Mennonite Life in the Twentieth Century*. Edited by Myrna Burkholder. Elkhart, IN: Institute of Mennonite Studies, 2016.

Burkholder, John Richard, and Barbara Nelson Gingerich, eds. *Mennonite Peace Theology: A Panorama of Types*. Akron, PA: Mennonite Central Committee Peace Office, 1991.

Burrow, Rufus, Jr. *Extremist for Love: Martin Luther King Jr., Man of Ideas and Nonviolent Social Action*. Minneapolis: Fortress, 2014.

———. *God and Human Dignity: The Personalism, Theology, and Ethics of Martin Luther King, Jr.* Notre Dame, IN: University of Notre Dame Press, 2006.

Cahill, Lisa Sowle. *Blessed Are the Peacemakers: Pacifism, Just War, and Peacebuilding*. Minneapolis: Fortress, 2019.

———. "A Church for Peace: Why Just-War Theory Isn't Enough." *Commonweal*, July 11, 2016, 9–13.

———. *Love Your Enemies: Discipleship, Pacifism, and Just War Theory.* Minneapolis: Fortress, 1994.

———. "A Theology for Peacebuilding." In *Peacebuilding: Catholic Theology, Ethics, and Praxis,* edited by Robert J. Schreiter, R. Scott Appleby, and Gerard F. Powers, 300–331. Maryknoll, NY: Orbis Books, 2010.

Câmara, Hélder. *The Church and Colonialism: The Betrayal of the Third World.* Translated by William McSweeney. Denville, NJ: Dimension, 1969.

———. *Dom Hélder Câmara: Essential Writings.* Selected with an introduction by Francis McDonagh. Maryknoll, NY: Orbis Books, 2009.

———. *Hoping against All Hope.* Translated by Matthew J. O'Connell. Quezon City, Philippines: Claretian, 1984.

———. *Questions for Living.* Translated by Robert R. Barr. Maryknoll, NY: Orbis Books, 1987.

———. *Revolution through Peace.* Edited by Ruth Nanda Anshen. Translated by Amparo McLean. World Perspectives 45. New York: Harper & Row, 1971.

———. *Spiral of Violence.* Translated by Della Couling. London: Sheed and Ward, 1971.

Camosy, Charles. *For the Love of Animals: Christian Ethics, Consistent Action.* Cincinnati: Franciscan Media, 2013.

Camp, Lee C. *Mere Discipleship: Radical Christianity in a Rebellious World.* 2nd ed. Grand Rapids: Brazos, 2008.

Capizzi, Joseph E. *Politics, Justice and War: Christian Governance and the Ethics of Warfare.* New York: Oxford University Press, 2015.

Carnes, Natalie. "A Reconsideration of Religious Authority in Christian Theology." *Heythrop Journal* 55 (2014): 467–80.

Chalamet, Christophe. *Revivalism and Social Christianity: The Prophetic Faith of Henri Nick and André Trocmé.* Eugene, OR: Pickwick, 2013.

Chenoweth, Erica, and Maria J. Stephan. *Why Civil Resistance Works: The Strategic Logic of Nonviolent Conflict.* New York: Columbia University Press, 2011.

Childress, James F. *Civil Disobedience and Political Obligation: A Study in Christian Social Ethics.* New Haven, CT: Yale University Press, 1971.

Claiborne, Shane, and Michael Martin. *Beating Guns: Hope for People Who Are Weary of Violence.* Grand Rapids: Brazos, 2019.

Clark, Patrick. "Is Martyrdom Virtuous? An Occasion for Rethinking the Relation of Christ and Virtue in Aquinas." *Journal of the Society of Christian Ethics* 30 (2010): 141–59.

Cochran, David Carroll. *Catholic Realism and the Abolition of War*. Maryknoll, NY: Orbis Books, 2014.

Colaiaco, James A. *Martin Luther King, Jr.: Apostle of Militant Nonviolence*. New York: St. Martin's Press, 1988.

Colón-Emeric, Edgardo. *Óscar Romero's Theological Vision: Liberation and the Transfiguration of the Poor*. South Bend, IN: University of Notre Dame Press, 2018.

Cone, James. *God of the Oppressed*. 2nd ed. Maryknoll, NY: Orbis Books, 1997.

Cortright, David. *Peace: A History of Movements and Ideas*. New York: Cambridge University Press, 2008.

Cramer, David C. "Evangelical Hermeneutics, Anabaptist Ethics: John Howard Yoder, the *Solas*, and the Question of War." In *The Activist Impulse: Essays on the Intersection of Anabaptism and Evangelicalism*, edited by Jared S. Burkholder and David C. Cramer, 379–405. Eugene, OR: Pickwick, 2012.

———. "A Field Guide to Christian Nonviolence." *Sojourners*, January 1, 2016, 31–35.

———. "Mennonites & Pacifism: The Mennonite Peace Witness across the Spectrum." *The Mennonite*, July 2017, 18–21.

———. "Realistic Transformation: The Impact of the Niebuhr Brothers on the Social Ethics of John Howard Yoder." *Mennonite Quarterly Review* 88 (2014): 479–515.

———. "Theopolitics: The Theological Lineage of Walter Rauschenbusch, Reinhold Niebuhr, and John Howard Yoder." PhD diss., Baylor University, 2016.

Cramer, David C., Jenny Howell, Paul Martens, and Jonathan Tran. "Theology and Misconduct: The Case of John Howard Yoder." *Christian Century*, August 20, 2014, 20–23.

Dandelion, Pink. *The Quakers: A Very Short Introduction*. Oxford: Oxford University Press, 2008.

Day, Dorothy. "Fight Conscription." *Catholic Worker*, September 1939, 1.

———. *From Union Square to Rome*. Maryknoll, NY: Orbis Books, 2006.

———. *Houses of Hospitality*. London: Sheed and Ward, 1939.

Dear, John. *Disarming the Heart: Toward a Vow of Nonviolence.* Scottdale, PA: Herald, 1993.

———. *The God of Peace: Toward a Theology of Nonviolence.* Maryknoll, NY: Orbis Books, 1994.

———. *Peace behind Bars: A Peacemaking Priest's Journal from Jail.* Franklin, WI: Sheed and Ward, 1995.

———, ed. *The Road to Peace: Writings on Peace and Justice.* Maryknoll, NY: Orbis Books, 1998.

———. *The Sacrament of Civil Disobedience.* Baltimore: Fortkamp, 1994.

———. *They Will Inherit the Earth: Peace and Nonviolence in a Time of Climate Change.* Maryknoll, NY: Orbis Books, 2018.

"Declaration of the International Meeting of Latin American Bishops on 'Nonviolence: A Power for Liberation,' November 28–December 3, 1977." Appendix A in Pérez Esquivel, *Christ in a Poncho,* 118–34.

DeJonge, Michael. *Bonhoeffer on Resistance: The Word against the Wheel.* Oxford: Oxford University Press, 2018.

Dekar, Paul. *Creating the Beloved Community: A Journey with the Fellowship of Reconciliation.* Kitchener, ON: Pandora, 2011.

Desmond, William. "Consecrating Peace: Reflecting on Daniel Berrigan and Witness." In *Faith, Resistance, and the Future: Daniel Berrigan's Challenge to Catholic Social Teaching,* edited by James L. Marsh and Anna J. Brown, 100–118. New York: Fordham University Press, 2012.

Dickinson, Roger. "Rauschenbusch and Niebuhr: Brothers under the Skin." *Religion in Life* 27, no. 2 (1958): 163–71.

Dixie, Quinton, and Peter Eisenstadt. *Visions of a Better World: Howard Thurman's Pilgrimage to India and the Origins of African American Nonviolence.* Boston: Beacon, 2011.

Dorrien, Gary. "King and His Mentors." *Commonweal* 144 (16): 17–21.

Douglas, Mark. *Christian Pacifism for an Environmental Age.* New York: Cambridge University Press, 2019.

Driedger, Leo, and Donald B. Kraybill. *Mennonite Peacemaking: From Quietism to Activism.* Scottdale, PA: Herald, 1994.

Ellul, Jacques. *Apocalypse: The Book of Revelation.* New York: Seabury, 1977.

———. *The New Demons.* Translated by C. Edward Hopkin. New York: Seabury, 1975.

———. *The Presence of the Kingdom.* Translated by Olive Wyon. New York: Seabury, 1967.

————. *Violence: Reflections from a Christian Perspective*. Translated by Cecelia Gaul Kings. New York: Seabury, 1970.

Evans, Christopher. *The Kingdom Is Always but Coming: A Life of Walter Rauschenbusch*. Waco: Baylor University Press, 2010.

————. "Ties That Bind: Walter Rauschenbusch, Reinhold Niebuhr, and the Quest for Economic Justice." *Soundings: An Interdisciplinary Journal* 95 (2012): 351–69.

Fiorenza, Elisabeth Schüssler, and Mary Shawn Copeland, eds. *Violence against Women*. Concilium. Maryknoll, NY: Orbis Books, 1994.

Firnhaber-Baker, Justine. "From God's Peace to the King's Order: Late Medieval Limitations on Non-Royal Warfare." *Essays in Medieval Studies* 23 (2006): 19–30.

Ford, J. Massyngbaerde. *My Enemy Is My Guest: Jesus and Violence in Luke*. Maryknoll, NY: Orbis Books, 1984.

Fortune, Marie Marshall. *Is Nothing Sacred? When Sex Invades the Pastoral Relationship*. New York: Harper & Row, 1989.

————. *Love Does No Harm: Sexual Ethics for the Rest of Us*. New York: Continuum, 1995.

————. *Sexual Violence: The Sin Revisited*. Cleveland: Pilgrim, 2005.

————. *Sexual Violence: The Unmentionable Sin*. New York: Pilgrim, 1983.

Francis (pope). *Angelus*. Vatican Library. August 18, 2013. https://www.vatican.va/content/francesco/en/angelus/2013/documents/papa-francesco_angelus_20130818.html.

————. "Nonviolence: A Style of Politics for Peace." Vatican Library. January 1, 2017. http://www.vatican.va/content/francesco/en/messages/peace/documents/papa-francesco_20161208_messaggio-l-giornata-mondiale-pace-2017.html.

Friesen, Duane K. *Christian Peacemaking and International Conflict: A Realist Pacifist Perspective*. Scottdale, PA: Herald, 1986.

————. "On Doing Social Ethics: A Personal Response." In *The Limits of Perfection: A Conversation with J. Lawrence Burkholder*, 2nd ed, edited by Rodney J. Sawatsky and Scott Holland, 127–34. Kitchener, ON: Pandora, 1993.

Gandolfo, Elizabeth O'Donnell. "Motherhood, Violence, and Peacemaking: A Practical-Theological Lesson from Liberia." In *Violence, Transformation, and the Sacred: "They Shall Be Called Children of God,"* edited by Margaret R. Pfeil and Tobias L. Winright, 160–74. Maryknoll, NY: Orbis Books, 2012.

Garvy, Michael O. "In Memoriam: Josephine Massyngbaerde Ford, professor emerita of theology at Notre Dame." *Notre Dame News.* May 20, 2015. https://news.nd.edu/news/in-memoriam-josephine-massyngbaerde-ford-professor-emerita-of-theology-at-notre-dame.

Gbowee, Leymah, with Carol Mithers. *Mighty Be Our Powers: How Sisterhood, Prayer, and Sex Changed a Nation at War; A Memoir.* New York: Beast, 2011.

Gelderloos, Peter. *How Nonviolence Protects the State.* Boston: South End, 2007.

Girard, René. "Mimesis and Violence." In *The Girard Reader*, edited by James G. Williams, 9–19. New York: Herder and Herder, 1996.

———. *Things Hidden since the Foundation of the World.* Stanford: Stanford University Press, 1987.

Goossen, Rachel Waltner, "'Defanging the Beast': Mennonite Responses to John Howard Yoder's Sexual Abuse." *Mennonite Quarterly Review* 89 (2015): 7–80.

Gorman, Michael J. *Becoming the Gospel: Paul, Participation, and Mission.* Grand Rapids: Eerdmans, 2015.

———. *Inhabiting the Cruciform God: Kenosis, Justification, and Theosis in Paul's Narrative Soteriology.* Grand Rapids: Eerdmans, 2009.

Graber, Barbra. "What's to Be Done about John Howard Yoder?" *Survivors Standing Tall*, July 17, 2013, https://www.survivorsstandingtall.org/single-post/2017/12/29/whats-to-be-done-about-john-howard-yoder.

Gregg, Richard. *The Power of Nonviolence.* Ahmedabad: Navajivan House, 1949.

Gutiérrez, Gustavo. *A Theology of Liberation: History, Politics, and Salvation.* Rev. ed. Maryknoll, NY: Orbis Books, 1988.

Hallie, Philip P. *Lest Innocent Blood Be Shed: The Story of the Village of Le Chambon and How Goodness Happened There.* New York: Harper Collins, 1994.

Hamer, Fannie Lou. *The Speeches of Fannie Lou Hamer: To Tell It Like It Is.* Edited by Maegan Parker Brooks and Davis W. Houck. Oxford, MS: University Press of Mississippi, 2013.

Haring, Bernard. *Christian Renewal in a Changing World.* Translated by Sister M. Lucidia Haring. Garden City, NY: Image, 1968.

———. *The Healing Power of Peace and Nonviolence.* Mahwah, NJ: Paulist Press, 1986.

———. *The Law of Christ*. Translated by Edwin G. Kaiser. Westminster, MD: Newman, 1964.

Harkness, Georgia. *Christian Ethics*. Nashville: Abingdon, 1957.

———. *The Ministry of Reconciliation*. Nashville: Abingdon, 1971.

———. *The Sources of Western Morality: From Punitive Society through the Beginnings of Christianity*. New York: Charles Scribner's Sons, 1954.

———. "A Spiritual Pilgrimage." *Christian Century*, March 15, 1939, 348–51.

Harnack, Adolf von. *Militia Christi: The Christian Religion and the Military in the First Three Centuries*. Philadelphia: Fortress, 1981.

Harvey, Barry. *Taking Hold of the Real: Dietrich Bonhoeffer and the Profound Worldliness of Christianity*. Eugene, OR: Cascade Books, 2015.

Hauerwas, Stanley. *Approaching the End: Eschatological Reflections on Church, Politics, and Life*. Grand Rapids: Eerdmans, 2013.

———. *Character and the Christian Life: A Study in Theological Ethics*. Notre Dame, IN: University of Notre Dame Press, 1994.

———. *The Character of Virtue: Letters to a Godson*. Grand Rapids: Eerdmans, 2018.

———. *A Community of Character: Toward a Constructive Christian Social Ethic*. Notre Dame, IN: University of Notre Dame Press, 1981.

———. *The Peaceable Kingdom: A Primer in Christian Ethics*. Notre Dame, IN: University of Notre Dame Press, 1983.

———. *Performing the Faith: Bonhoeffer and the Practice of Nonviolence*. Grand Rapids: Brazos, 2004.

———. *Sanctify Them in the Truth: Holiness Exemplified*. New York: T&T Clark, 1998.

———. *With the Grain of the Universe: The Church's Witness and Natural Theology*. Grand Rapids: Brazos, 2001.

Hauerwas, Stanley, and Charles Pinches. *Christians among the Virtues: Theological Conversations with Ancient and Modern Ethics*. Notre Dame, IN: University of Notre Dame Press, 1997.

Hays, Richard. *The Moral Vision of the New Testament: A Contemporary Introduction to New Testament Ethics*. San Francisco: HarperSanFrancisco, 1996.

Head, Thomas. "The Development of the Peace of God in Aquitaine (970–1005)." *Speculum* 74, no. 3 (July 1999): 656–86.

Heggen, Carolyn Holderread. *Sexual Abuse in Christian Homes and Churches*. Scottdale, PA: Herald, 1993.

Helgeland, John, Robert J. Daly, and J. Patout Burns. *Christians and the Military: The Early Experience*. Philadelphia: Fortress: 1985.

Hershberger, Guy F. "Pacifism and the State in Colonial Pennsylvania." *Church History* 8 (1939): 54–74.

Hill, Johnny Bernard. *The Theology of Martin Luther King, Jr. and Desmond Mpilo Tutu*. New York: Palgrave Macmillan, 2007.

Holsaert, Faith S., Martha Prescod Norman Noonan, Judy Richardson, Betty Garman Robinson, Jean Smith Young, and Dorothy M. Zellner, eds. *Hands on the Freedom Plow: Personal Accounts by the Women of SNCC*. Champaign: University of Illinois Press, 2010.

Hunter-Bowman, Janna L. "Constructive Agents under Duress: Alternatives to the Structural, Political, and Agential Inadequacies of Past Theologies of Nonviolent Peacebuilding Efforts." *Journal of the Society of Christian Ethics* 38, no. 2 (2018): 149–68.

———. "Peace through Participation: Enhancing Post-accord Peacebuilding through Linking Stakeholders to Peace Accord Stipulations." *Journal of Peacebuilding & Development* 14, no. 1 (2019): 68–72.

Insko, Jeffrey. *History, Abolition, and the Ever-Present Now in Antebellum American Writing*. New York: Oxford University Press, 2019.

Jantzen, Grace. *Violence to Eternity*. Edited by Jeremy Carrette and Morny Joy. New York: Routledge, 2009.

John XXIII (pope). *Pacem in Terris* [Encyclical of Pope John XXIII on Establishing Universal Peace in Truth, Justice, Charity, and Liberty]. Vatican Library. April 11, 1963. http://www.vatican.va/content/john-xxiii/en/encyclicals/documents/hf_j-xxiii_enc_11041963_pacem.html.

Kalantzis, George. *Caesar and the Lamb: Early Christian Attitudes on War and Military Service*. Eugene, OR: Cascade Books, 2012.

Käsemann, Ernst. *Church Conflicts: The Cross, Apocalyptic, and Political Resistance*. Edited by Ry O. Siggelkow. Grand Rapids: Baker Academic, 2021.

Katz, Milton. *Ban the Bomb: A History of SANE, The Committee for a Sane Nuclear Policy, 1957–1985*. Westport, CT: Praeger, 1987.

Keller, Rosemary Skinner. *Georgia Harkness: For Such a Time as This*. Nashville: Abingdon, 1992.

King, Martin Luther, Jr. "Beyond Vietnam." In *A Call to Conscience: The Landmark Speeches of Martin Luther King, Jr.*, edited by Clayborne Carson, 133–64. New York: IPM/Warner, 2001.

———. "Letter from Birmingham Jail." In West, *Radical King*, 127–46.

———. "My Pilgrimage to Nonviolence." In West, *Radical King*, 55–72.

———. "The Revolution of Nonviolent Resistance." In West, *Radical King*, 147–54.

———. *A Testament of Hope: The Essential Writings and Speeches of Martin Luther King, Jr.* Edited by James M. Washington. San Francisco: HarperSanFrancisco, 1986.

Kosek, Joseph Kip. *Acts of Conscience: Christian Nonviolence and Modern American Democracy.* New York: Columbia University Press, 2009.

Krall, Ruth Elizabeth. *The Elephant in God's Living Room.* 4 vols. N.p.: Enduring Space, 2012.

———. "John Howard Yoder: An Annotated Timeline." *Enduring Space.* January 15, 2015. https://ruthkrall.com/jhy-biblio/john-howard-yoder-an-annotated-timeline-amended-2015.

Krauss, Clifford. "U.S., Aware of Killings, Worked with Salvador's Rightists, Papers Suggest." *New York Times*, November 9, 1993, A1, 9.

Krehbiel, Stephanie Joan. "Pacifist Battlegrounds: Violence, Community, and the Struggle for LGBTQ Justice in the Mennonite Church USA." PhD diss., Kansas University, 2015.

Larry, Susannah. *Leaving Silence: Sexualized Violence, the Bible, and Standing with Survivors.* Harrisonburg, VA: Herald, 2021.

Lederach, John Paul. *Building Peace: Sustainable Reconciliation in Divided Societies.* Washington, DC: US Institute of Peace Press, 1997.

———. *The Moral Imagination: The Art and Soul of Building Peace.* New York: Oxford University Press, 2005.

———. *Preparing for Peace: Conflict Transformation across Cultures.* Syracuse, NY: Syracuse University Press, 1996.

Lee, Michael E. *Revolutionary Saint: The Theological Legacy of Oscar Romero.* Maryknoll, NY: Orbis Books, 2018.

Lehmann, Paul. *The Transfiguration of Politics: The Presence and Power of Jesus of Nazareth in and over Human Affairs.* New York: Harper & Row, 1975.

León, Luis D. *The Political Spirituality of Cesar Chavez: Crossing Religious Borders.* Berkeley: University of California Press, 2015.

Lewy, Geunter. *Peace and Revolution: The Moral Crisis of American Pacifism.* Grand Rapids: Eerdmans, 1988.

Lloyd, Vincent. *Black Natural Law.* Oxford: Oxford University Press, 2016.

Lovin, Robin W. *Christian Realism and the New Realities.* New York: Cambridge University Press, 2008.

———. *Reinhold Niebuhr and Christian Realism*. New York: Cambridge University Press, 1995.

Lozano, Alix. "Women of Faith Advocating Peace in Colombia." In *Liberating the Politics of Jesus: Renewing Peace Theology through the Wisdom of Women*, edited by Elizabeth Soto Albrecht and Darryl W. Stephens, 82–95. New York: T&T Clark, 2020.

Luciani, Rafael. "Medellín Fifty Years Later: From Development to Liberation." *Theological Studies* 79 (2018): 566–89.

Marshall, Ellen Ott. *Christians in the Public Square: Faith That Transforms Politics*. Nashville: Abingdon, 2008.

Martens, Paul. "With the Grain of the Universe: Reexamining the Alleged Nonviolent Rejection of Natural Law." *Journal of the Society of Christian Ethics* 32 (2012): 113–31.

Mast, Gerald J., and J. Denny Weaver. *Defenseless Christianity: Anabaptism for a Nonviolent Church*. Telford, PA: Cascadia, 2009.

McCarthy, Eli. *Becoming Nonviolent Peacemakers: A Virtue Ethic for Catholic Social Teaching and U.S. Policy*. Eugene, OR: Wipf & Stock, 2012.

McCarty, James. "Nonviolent Law? Linking Nonviolent Social Change and Truth and Reconciliation Commissions." *West Virginia Law Review* 114, no. 3 (2012): 969–1005.

McDonagh, Francis. Introduction to *Dom Hélder Câmara*, by Câmara, 11–36.

McKnight, Scot. *Kingdom Conspiracy: Returning to the Radical Mission of the Local Church*. Grand Rapids: Brazos, 2014.

———. *Reading Romans Backwards: A Gospel of Peace in the Midst of Empire*. Waco: Baylor University Press, 2019.

———. *The Sermon on the Mount*. The Story of God Bible Commentary. Grand Rapids: Zondervan Academic, 2013.

McManus, Philip, and Gerald Schlabach, eds. *Relentless Persistence: Nonviolent Action in Latin America*. Philadelphia: New Society, 1991.

Meilaender, Gilbert C. *The Theory and Practice of Virtue*. Notre Dame, IN: University of Notre Dame Press, 1984.

Merton, Thomas. "Blessed Are the Meek: The Christian Roots of Nonviolence." In Shannon, *Passion for Peace*, 248–59.

———. "Christian Action in World Crisis." In Shannon, *Passion for Peace*, 80–92.

———. "The Christian as Peacemaker." In *Peace in the Post-Christian Era*, edited by Patricia A. Burton, 27–33. Maryknoll, NY: Orbis Books, 2004.

———. *Faith and Violence: Christian Teaching and Christian Practice.* Notre Dame, IN: University of Notre Dame Press, 1968.

———. *Gandhi on Nonviolence.* New York: New Directions, 1964.

———. "The Root of War Is Fear." In *Passion for Peace: The Social Essays,* edited by William H. Shannon, 11–19. New York: Crossroad, 2005.

———. *Signs of Peace: The Interfaith Letters of Thomas Merton.* Edited by William Apel. Maryknoll, NY: Orbis Books, 2013.

Micks, Marianne H. "Georgia Harkness: Chastened Liberal." *Theology Today* 53 (October 1996): 311–19.

Moskos, Charles C., and John Whiteclay Chambers II. *The New Conscientious Objectors: From Sacred to Secular Resistance.* Oxford: Oxford University Press, 1993.

Muste, A. J. *Of Holy Disobedience.* Lebanon, PA: Pendle Hill, 1952.

———. *Nonviolence in an Aggressive World.* New York: Harper & Brothers, 1940.

———. *Not by Might: Christianity, the Way of Human Decency.* New York: Harper & Brothers, 1947.

Nation, Mark Theissen, Anthony G. Siegrist, and Daniel Umbel. *Bonhoeffer the Assassin? Challenging the Myth, Recovering His Call to Peacemaking.* Grand Rapids: Baker Academic, 2013.

National [US] Conference of Catholic Bishops. *The Challenge of Peace: God's Promise and Our Response.* Washington, DC: USCC Office for Publishing and Promotion Services, 1983. https://www.usccb.org/upload/challenge-peace-gods-promise-our-response-1983.pdf.

———. "The Harvest of Justice Is Sown in Peace." November 17, 1993. https://www.usccb.org/resources/harvest-justice-sown-peace.

Nepstad, Sharon Erickson. *Nonviolent Revolutions: Civil Resistance in the Late 20th Century.* Oxford: Oxford University Press, 2011.

———. *Religion and War Resistance in the Plowshares Movement.* New York: Cambridge University Press, 2008.

Niebuhr, Reinhold. *An Interpretation of Christian Ethics.* New York: Harper & Brothers, 1935.

———. "Walter Rauschenbusch in Historical Perspective." In *Faith and Politics,* edited by Ronald Stone, 33–45. New York: Braziller, 1968.

———. "Why the Christian Church Is Not Pacifist." In *War in the Twentieth Century: Sources in Theological Ethics,* edited by Richard B. Miller, 28–46. Louisville: Westminster John Knox, 1992.

Nixon, Rob. *Slow Violence and the Environmentalism of the Poor*. Cambridge, MA: Harvard University Press, 2011.

Nouwen, Henri. "Celebrating Life." In Dear, *Road to Peace*, 40–55.

———. *¡Gracias! A Latin American Journal*. Maryknoll, NY: Orbis Books, 1983.

———. "No to Vietnam." In Dear, *Road to Peace*, 67–68.

———. *The Path of Power*. New York: Crossroad, 1995.

———. *Peacework: Prayer, Resistance, Community*. Maryknoll, NY: Orbis Books, 2014.

———. *The Selfless Way of Christ: Downward Mobility and the Spiritual Life*. Maryknoll, NY: Orbis Books, 2007.

Nussburger, Danielle. "Vegetarianism: A Christian Spiritual Practice Both Old and New." In York and Alexis-Baker, *Faith Embracing All Creatures*, 166–80.

O'Brien, Kevin J. *The Violence of Climate Change: Lessons of Resistance from Nonviolent Activists*. Washington, DC: Georgetown University Press, 2017.

O'Brien, Tim. *The Things They Carried*. New York: Houghton Mifflin, 1990.

O'Donovan, Oliver. *The Just War Revisited*. New York: Cambridge University Press, 2003.

Olsson, Göran Hugo, dir. *The Black Power Mixtape 1967–1975*. New York: Louverture Films, 2011.

Origen. *Homilies of Joshua* 14.1. In Kalantzis, *Caesar and the Lamb*, 147.

Orosco, José-Antonio. *Cesar Chavez and the Common Sense of Nonviolence*. Albuquerque: University of New Mexico Press, 2008.

Paul VI (pope). *Gaudium et spes* [Pastoral Constitution on the Church in the Modern World]. Vatican Library. December 7, 1965. https://www.vatican.va/archive/hist_councils/ii_vatican_council/documents/vat-ii_cons_19651207_gaudium-et-spes_en.html.

———. *Populorum progressio* [Encyclical on the Development of Peoples]. Vatican Library. March 26, 1967. http://www.vatican.va/content/paul-vi/en/encyclicals/documents/hf_p-vi_enc_26031967_populorum.html.

Penner, Carol Jean. "Mennonite Silences and Feminist Voices: Peace Theology and Violence against Women." PhD diss., University of St. Michael's College, 1999.

Penner, Kimberly L. "Mennonite Peace Theology and Violence against Women." *Conrad Grebel Review* 35, no. 3 (2017): 280–92.

Pérez Esquivel, Adolfo. *Christ in a Poncho: Witnesses to the Nonviolent Struggles in Latin America*. Edited by Charles Antoine. Translated by Robert R. Barr. Maryknoll, NY: Orbis Books, 1983.

Porter, Jean. "Virtue." In *The Oxford Handbook of Theological Ethics*, edited by Gilbert Meilaender and William Werpehowski, 205–20. Oxford: Oxford University Press, 2005.

Prevot, Andrew. *Thinking Prayer: Theology and Spirituality amid the Crises of Modernity*. Notre Dame, IN: University of Notre Dame Press, 2015.

Rauschenbusch, Walter. *Christianity and the Social Crisis in the 21st Century: The Classic That Woke Up the Church*. New York: HarperOne, 2007. First published 1907 as *Christianity and the Social Crisis*.

———. *The Righteousness of the Kingdom*. Edited by Max. L. Stackhouse. Nashville: Abingdon, 1968.

———. *The Social Principles of Jesus*. New York: The International Committee of Young Men's Christian Association, 1916.

———. *A Theology for the Social Gospel*. Louisville: Westminster John Knox, 1997. First published 1917.

Rauschenbusch, Walter, and Charles Aked. "Private Profit and the Nation's Honor: A Protest and a Plea." July 8, 1915, four-page leaflet, https://www.patheos.com/blogs/anabaptistrevisions/2020/01/private-profit-nations-honor.

Reticker, Gini, dir. *Pray the Devil Back to Hell*. Amherst, MA: Balcony Releasing, 2008. DVD.

Robbins, Anna M. *Methods in the Madness: Diversity in Twentieth-Century Christian Social Ethics*. Carlisle, UK: Paternoster, 2004.

Roberts, J. Deotis. *Liberation and Reconciliation: A Black Theology*. 2nd ed. Louisville: Westminster John Knox, 2005.

Rohr, John A. *Prophets without Honor: Public Policy and the Selective Conscientious Objector*. Nashville: Abingdon, 1971.

Romero, Óscar. *Voice of the Voiceless: The Four Pastoral Letters and Other Statements*. Translated by Michael J. Walsh. Maryknoll, NY: Orbis Books, 1985.

Rutschman, LaVerne A. "Anabaptism and Liberation Theology." In Schipani, *Freedom and Discipleship*, 51–65.

Rutter, Peter. *Sex in the Forbidden Zone: When Men in Power—Therapists, Doctors, Clergy, Teachers, and Others—Betray Women's Trust*. Los Angeles: Tarcher, 1989.

Sattler, Michael. "The Schleitheim Articles." In *The Radical Reformation*, edited by Michael Baylor, 172–80. New York: Cambridge University Press, 1991.

Scarsella, Hilary Jerome, and Stephanie Krehbiel. "Sexual Violence: Christian Theological Legacies." *Religion Compass* 13 (2019): 1–13.

Scheid, Anna Floerke. *Just Revolution: A Christian Ethic of Political Resistance and Social Transformation*. Lanham, MD: Lexington, 2015.

Schipani, Daniel S., ed. *Freedom and Discipleship: Liberation Theology in an Anabaptist Perspective*. Maryknoll, NY: Orbis Books, 1989.

Schipani, Daniel S., and Anton Wessels, eds. *The Promise of Hope: A Tribute to Dom Hélder*. Elkhart, IN: Institute of Mennonite Studies, 2002.

Schlabach, Gerald W. "Just Policing and the Christian Call to Nonviolence." In *At Peace and Unafraid: Public Order, Security, and the Wisdom of the Cross*, edited by Duane K. Friesen and Gerald W. Schlabach, 405–21. Scottdale, PA: Herald, 2005.

———, ed. *Just Policing, Not War: An Alternative Response to World Violence*. Collegeville, MN: Liturgical Press, 2007.

———. "Just the Police Function, Then: A Response to 'The Gospel or a Glock?'" *Conrad Grebel Review* 26, no. 2 (2008): 50–60.

———. "Must Christian Pacifists Reject Police Force?" In *A Faith Not Worth Fighting For: Addressing Commonly Asked Questions about Christian Nonviolence*, edited by Tripp York and Justin Bronson Barringer, 60–84. Eugene, OR: Cascade Books, 2012.

———. *A Pilgrim People: Becoming a Catholic Peace Church*. Collegeville, MN: Liturgical Press, 2019.

Schoenborn, Paul Gerhard. "Oscar Arnulfo Romero: The Defender of the Poor." In *Christianity and Resistance in the 20th Century: From Kaj Munk and Dietrich Bonhoeffer to Desmond Tutu*, edited by Søren Dosenrode, 233–60. Boston: Brill, 2008.

Schott, Hanna. *Love in a Time of Hate: The Story of Magda and André Trocmé and the Village That Said No to the Nazis*. Translated by John D. Roth. Harrisonburg, VA: Herald, 2017.

Selby, Gary S. *Martin Luther King and the Rhetoric of Freedom: The Exodus Narrative in America's Struggle for Civil Rights*. Waco: Baylor University Press, 2008.

Shannon, William H., ed. *Passion for Peace: The Social Essays*. New York: Crossroad, 1997.

Sharp, Gene. *Politics of Nonviolent Action*. Part 1, *Power and Struggle*. Boston: Porter Sargent, 1973.

———. *Politics of Nonviolent Action*. Part 2, *The Methods of Nonviolent Action*. Boston: Porter Sargent, 1973.

———. *Politics of Nonviolent Action*. Part 3, *The Dynamics of Nonviolent Action*. Boston: Porter Sargent, 1973.

Shean, John F. *Soldiering for God: Christianity and the Roman Army*. Leiden: Brill, 2010.

Sheldon, Charles Monroe. *In His Steps: What Would Jesus Do?* Chicago: Chicago Advance, 1896.

Shenk, Joanna. *The Movement Makes Us Human: An Interview with Dr. Vincent Harding on Mennonites, Vietnam, and MLK*. Eugene, OR: Wipf & Stock, 2018.

Sider, Ronald J. *Nonviolent Action: What Christian Ethics Demands but Most Christians Have Never Really Tried*. Grand Rapids: Brazos, 2015.

Siggelkow, Ry O. "Toward an Apocalyptic Peace Church: Christian Pacifism after Hauerwas." *Conrad Grebel Review* 31, no. 3 (2013): 274–97.

Smith, Shanell T. *Touched: For Survivors of Sexual Assault Like Me Who Have Been Hurt by Church Folk and for Those Who Will Care*. Minneapolis: Fortress, 2020.

Sölle, Dorothee. *The Arms Race Kills Even without War*. Philadelphia: Fortress, 1983.

———. *The Strength of the Weak: Toward a Christian Feminist Identity*. Philadelphia: Westminster, 1984.

———. *Suffering*. Philadelphia: Fortress, 1975.

Sprinkle, Preston. *Fight: A Christian Case for Nonviolence*. Colorado Springs: David C. Cook, 2013.

Stackhouse, Max L. "Eschatology and Ethical Method: A Structural Analysis of Christian Social Ethics in America with Primary Reference to Walter Rauschenbusch and Reinhold Niebuhr." PhD diss., Harvard University, 1964.

Stassen, Glen. "Holistic, Interactive Character Formation for Just Peacemaking." In *Formation for Life: Just Peacemaking and Twenty-First Century Discipleship*, edited by Glen H. Stassen, Rodney L. Petersen, and Timothy A. Norton, 3–28. Eugene, OR: Pickwick, 2013.

———, ed. *Just Peacemaking: Ten Practices for Abolishing War*. Cleveland: Pilgrim, 1998.

————. *Just Peacemaking: Transforming Initiatives for Justice and Peace.* Louisville: Westminster John Knox, 1992.

————. *Living the Sermon on the Mount: A Practical Hope for Grace and Deliverance.* San Francisco: Jossey-Bass, 2006.

Stone, Ronald H. "Realist Criticism of Just Peacemaking." *Journal of the Society of Christian Ethics* 23 (2003): 255–67.

Stringfellow, William. *An Ethic for Christians and Other Aliens in a Strange World.* Waco: Word, 1973.

————. "The Ethics of Violence." *Cross Beat,* March 1966, 3–6.

————. *Free in Obedience.* New York: Seabury, 1967.

————. *Imposters of God: Inquiries into Favorite Idols.* Washington, DC: Witness, 1969.

————. *A Keeper of the Word: Selected Writings of William Stringfellow.* Edited by Bill Wylie-Kellerman. Grand Rapids: Eerdmans, 1994.

————. *A Second Birthday: A Personal Confrontation with Illness, Pain, and Death.* New York: Doubleday, 1970.

Stringfellow, William, and Anthony Towne. *Suspect Tenderness: The Ethics of the Berrigan Witness.* Canada: Holt, Rinehart & Winston, 1971.

Sullivan, Dennis, and Fred Boehrer, "The Practice of Nonviolence in the Contemporary World: An Interview with Daniel Berrigan." *Contemporary Justice Review* 5 (2002): 53–61.

Swartley, Willard M. *Covenant of Peace: The Missing Peace in New Testament Theology and Ethics.* Grand Rapids: Eerdmans, 2006.

Swift, Louis. *Early Fathers on War and Military Service.* Collegeville, MN: Glazier, 1983.

Thistlethwaite, Susan Brooks. *Women's Bodies as Battlefield: Christian Theology and the Global War on Women.* New York: Palgrave Macmillan, 2015.

Thomas, Leah R. *Just Care: Ethical Anti-Racist Pastoral Care with Women with Mental Illness.* Lanham, MD: Lexington Books / Fortress Academic, 2020.

Thomas Aquinas. *Summa Theologica* II-II. Translated by Fathers of the English Dominican Province. Westminster, MD: Christian Classics, 1981.

Thurman, Howard. *The Creative Encounter.* New York: Harper & Brothers, 1954.

————. *Deep Is the Hunger: Meditations.* New York: Harper & Row, 1951.

————. *The Growing Edge: Sermons in Worship Patterns.* New York: Harper & Brothers, 1956.

———. *Jesus and the Disinherited*. Boston: Beacon, 1976.

———. *The Luminous Darkness: A Personal Interpretation of the Anatomy of Segregation and the Ground of Hope*. New York: Harper & Row, 1965.

———. *Meditations of the Heart*. Boston: Beacon, 1999.

———. "Mysticism and Social Change." In *The Papers of Howard Washington Thurman*. Vol. 2, *Christian, Who Calls Me Christian?*, 190–221. Columbia: University of South Carolina Press, 2012.

———. "The Significance of Jesus." In *The Papers of Howard Washington Thurman*. Vol. 2, *Christian, Who Calls Me Christian?*, 85–90. Columbia: University of South Carolina Press, 2012.

Trocmé, André. *Jesus and the Nonviolent Revolution*. 2nd ed. Edited by Charles E. Moore. Walden, NY: Plough, 2003.

Troeltsch, Ernst. *The Social Teachings of the Christian Churches*. Vol. 2. Louisville: Westminster John Knox, 1992.

Tutu, Desmond. *God Has a Dream: A Vision of Hope for Our Time*. New York: Doubleday, 2004.

———. *The Nobel Peace Prize Lecture: Desmond Tutu*. New York: Phelps-Stokes Fund, 1986.

Villegas, Isaac Samuel. "The Ecclesial Ethics of John Howard Yoder's Abuse." *Modern Theology* (2020): 191–214.

Wadell, Paul J. *Happiness and the Christian Life: An Introduction to Christian Ethics*. Lanham, MD: Rowman & Littlefield, 2016.

Weil, Simone. *Gravity and Grace*. New York: Octagon, 1983.

Wells, Samuel, and Marcia A. Owen. *Living without Enemies: Being Present in the Midst of Violence*. Downers Grove, IL: IVP Books, 2011.

Wennberg, Robert N. *God, Humans and Animals: An Invitation to Enlarge Our Moral Universe*. Grand Rapids: Eerdmans, 2003.

Werntz, Myles. *Bodies of Peace: Ecclesiology, Nonviolence, and Witness*. Minneapolis: Fortress, 2014.

———. "Erase This from the Blackboard: Pearl Jam, John Howard Yoder, and the Overcoming of Violence." In *Secular Music and Sacred Theology*, edited by Tom Beaudoin, 108–25. Minneapolis: Liturgical Press, 2013.

———. "Ontology, Ecclesiology, Nonviolence: Resistance to War in the Thought of John Howard Yoder, Dorothy Day, and William Stringfellow." PhD diss., Baylor University, 2011.

———. "The Ubiquity of Christ and the Sites of Redemption: William Stringfellow, Ecclesiology and the Powers." *International Journal of Public Theology* 7, no. 3 (2013): 260–74.

———. "War in Christ's World: Bonhoeffer and Just Peacemaking on War and Christology." *Dialog: A Journal of Theology* 50 (2011): 90–96.

West, Traci C. *Disruptive Christian Ethics: When Racism and Women's Lives Matter.* Louisville: Westminster John Knox, 2006.

———. *Solidarity and Defiant Spirituality: Africana Lessons on Religion, Racism, and Ending Gender Violence.* New York: New York University Press, 2019.

———. *Wounds of the Spirit: Black Women, Violence, and Resistance Ethics.* New York: New York University Press, 1999.

Whelan, Matthew Philipp. *Blood in the Fields: Óscar Romero, Catholic Social Teaching, and Land Reform.* Washington, DC: Catholic University of America Press, 2020.

———. "'You Possess the Land That Belongs to All Salvadorans': Archbishop Óscar Romero and Ordinary Violence." *Modern Theology* 35, no. 4 (2019): 638–62.

Williams, Rowan. *The Truce of God.* Grand Rapids: Eerdmans, 2005.

Wink, Walter. *Naming the Powers.* Philadelphia: Fortress, 1987.

Yoder, Elizabeth G. *Peace Theology and Violence against Women.* Occasional Papers 16. Elkhart, IN: Institute of Mennonite Studies, 1992.

Yoder, John Howard. *Body Politics: Five Practices of the Christian Community before the Watching World.* Scottdale, PA: Herald, 2012. First published 1992.

———. *The Christian Witness to the State.* Scottdale, PA: Herald, 2002. First published 1964.

———. "The Hermeneutics of Peoplehood: A Protestant Perspective." In *The Priestly Kingdom: Social Ethics as Gospel,* 15–46. Notre Dame, IN: University of Notre Dame Press, 1984.

———. "The Nature of the Unity We Seek: A Free Church View." In *The Royal Priesthood: Essays Ecclesiastical and Ecumenical,* edited by Michael G. Cartwright, 221–30. Scottdale, PA: Herald, 1998.

———. *Nevertheless: The Varieties and Shortcomings of Religious Pacifism.* 2nd ed. Scottdale, PA: Herald, 1992. First published 1971.

———. *Nonviolence—A Brief History: The Warsaw Lectures.* Waco: Baylor University Press, 2010.

———. "The Otherness of the Church." In *The Royal Priesthood: Essays Ecclesiastical and Ecumenical,* edited by Michael G. Cartwright, 53–64. Scottdale, PA: Herald, 1998.

————. *The Politics of Jesus: Vicit Agnus Noster.* 2nd ed. Grand Rapids: Eerdmans, 1994. First published 1972.

————. *Revolutionary Christianity: The 1966 South American Lectures.* Edited by Paul Martens, Mark T. Nation, Matthew Porter, and Myles Werntz. Eugene, OR: Cascade Books, 2012.

York, Tripp, and Andy Alexis-Baker, eds. *A Faith Embracing All Creatures: Addressing Commonly Asked Questions about Christian Care for Animals.* Eugene, OR: Cascade Books, 2012.

Young, Andrew. *An Easy Burden: The Civil Rights Movement and the Transformation of America.* Waco: Baylor University Press, 2008.

Zehr, Howard. *The Little Book of Restorative Justice.* 2nd ed. New York: Good Books, 2015.

Ziegler, Philip G. *Militant Grace: The Apocalyptic Turn and the Future of Christian Theology.* Grand Rapids: Baker Academic, 2018.

INDEX

NRM

Non Relegious movement